Also by Michael C. Keith

Waves of Rancor (with Robert Hilliard)
The Hidden Screen (with Robert Hilliard)
Voices in the Purple Haze
Signals in the Air
Global Broadcasting Systems (with Robert Hilliard)
The Radio Station
The Broadcast Century (with Robert Hilliard)
Radio Programming
Selling Radio Direct
Broadcast Voice Performance
The Art and Science of Radio Production
Production in Format Radio

TALKING
RADIO

TALKING RADIO

An Oral History of American
Radio in the Television Age

Michael C. Keith

M.E.Sharpe
Armonk, New York
London, England

Library of Congress Cataloging-in-Publication Data

Talking radio: an oral history of American radio in the television age /
[edited by] Michael C. Keith.
p.   cm.
Includes bibliographical references and index.
ISBN 0–7656–0398–5 (alk. paper)
1. Radio broadcasting—United States—History. I. Keith, Michael C.
PN1991.2.T35   2000
384.54′0973—dc21   99–16230
CIP

Printed in the United States of America

The paper used in this publication meets the minimum requirements of
American National Standard for Information Sciences—
Permanence of Paper for Printed Library Materials,
ANSI Z 39.48-1984.

BM (c)   10   9   8   7   6   5   4   3   2   1

To Norman Corwin—Poet of air and waves

Radio introduced a new orality to American culture.
                                        —Susan J. Douglas

Contents

Part III. The Times and Bands Are A-Changin'

Part IV. Into the New Millennium

Preface

This is not a history per se of radio—at least not in the traditional sense. It does not aim to be conventionally comprehensive, but it does seek to be inclusive in its own chatty way. The reader should regard it as a well-informed discussion about post-World War II radio by the people who were instrumental in making radio history from around 1945 until the present (albeit, with occasional pre-war flashbacks for the sake of illustration and comparison). What takes place between these covers amounts to an exchange of perspectives concerning the role that radio has played in our society and culture since the arrival of television displaced it as the object of our attention in those long-ago evenings of the recently bygone millennium.

Why focus just on the second phase of radio's existence? The medium's golden age (ca. 1920–1950) has been the subject of numerous excellent retrospectives. There is an abundance of radio "heyday" studies—both serious and sentimental. For those interested in works mostly of the former kind, authors like Michele Hilmes, Gerald Nachman, Christopher Sterling, Leonard Maltin, John Kittross, Susan Douglas, Robert Hilliard (with me), Erik Barnouw, Tom Lewis, John Dunning, and J. Fred MacDonald do a very thorough and commendable job. So the ground has been covered well enough without my attempting to cover it again in this volume. (Incidentally, most of those authors just cited are contributors to this book.)

Talking Radio is an informal and intimate post-heyday review of radio—wherein nearly one hundred voices engage in a thoughtful and often provocative dialogue. Most of the participants in this colloquy have significant backgrounds in the aural medium and therefore are able to provide the reader with unique first-hand accounts of the central events and themes surrounding the evolution of radio since its gallant service in World War II.

Prominent, often legendary (over two dozen broadcast hall-of-famers), personalities, authors, scholars, and industry figures share their insiders' views and perspectives and provide a fresh and illuminating angle on a truly fascinating subject, especially for anyone interested in the interplay between mass media forms and their intended audiences and markets.

In all, there are twenty-four chapters (exchanges, if you will) on subjects of wide-ranging significance concerning radio following its initial incarnation as the nation's foremost home entertainment and information medium. Not all contributors celebrate the "remaking" of radio. In fact, there is much said in these pages to suggest that the medium has failed society since radio was forced to reinvent itself over half a century ago.

However, powerful evidence offered in these same pages indicates that radio has continued to serve its constituents with passion and brilliance to this very day.

Tune in and judge for yourself.

Acknowledgments

It has long been my hope and desire to engage as many legendary and prominent radio spokespeople as possible in the telling of the story of the audio medium after the fateful arrival of television. To that end, in spring 1998 (and truth be known, many years before), I began the task of sourcing and communicating with countless dozens of individuals who I felt could contribute unique and valuable insights and perspectives to this account. It goes without saying that those whose names appear in these pages represent but a fraction of the medium's eminent experts and professionals, but it is the author's opinion that it is a very formidable fraction indeed. It is to the one hundred voices recorded between these covers, as well as my family and friends and the ever sensitive and insightful staff at M.E. Sharpe—foremost among this stalwart cadre, Peter Coveney—that this book is also dedicated.

Cast of Contributors

*Steve Allen	Entertainer, author, and composer
Dave Archard	Deejay and advertising agency executive
LeRoy Bannerman	Academic, author, and biographer
Erik Barnouw	Historian, author, and dramatist
Marvin Bensman	Academic and industry expert
Peggy Berryhill	Producer, writer, and performer
Ed Bliss	News editor, producer, and writer
True Boardman	Entertainer and actor
Pierre Bouvard	Ratings company executive
Ray Bradbury	Novelist, essayist, and screenwriter
Frank Bresee	Entertainer and historian
*Himan Brown	Producer and industry executive
Jack Brown	Industry professional
Frank Chorba	Academic and journal editor
Lynn Christian	Industry executive and FM pioneer

*Hall of Famer: One who has been inducted into one or more of the following organizations: National Association of Broadcasters, Museum of Broadcast Communications, *Broadcasting and Cable Magazine*, and Museum of Television and Radio.

Several contributors are recipients of other major accolades as well, including the Pulitzer Prize, Tony Award, Grammy Award, Presidential Medal, and Golden Globe award, to mention only a few.

*Dick Clark	Entertainer and producer
Alan Colmes	Syndicated talk show host
Bud Connell	Industry and association executive
Bernarr Cooper	Actor and narrator
Joe Cortese	Deejay and syndicated host
*Norman Corwin	Writer, producer and director
*Walter Cronkite	News anchor, reporter, and writer
Blanquita Cullum	Syndicated talk-show host
Sam Dann	Writer and producer
*Rick Dees	Deejay and syndicated talk-show host
Rick Ducey	Association executive
John Dunning	Novelist and broadcast historian
Irving Fang	Academic, author, and news consultant
Dick Fatherley	Deejay and voice artist
James Fletcher	Academic and author
Corey Flintoff	News reporter, producer, and writer
*Stan Freberg	Entertainer, producer, and writer
*Larry Gelbart	Writer, producer, and humorist
Russ Gibb	Programmer and deejay
Arnie Ginsburg	Deejay and industry executive
Don Godfrey	Academic and author
Douglas Gomery	Academic and author
Lynne Gross	Academic and author
*Ralph Guild	Industry executive and pioneer
*Karl Haas	Syndicated host and music critic
Cecil Hale	Academic and industry expert
Donald Hall	Poet and author
Donna Halper	Consultant, academic, and author
Marty Halperin	Producer, audio technician, and historian
Michael Harrison	Industry publisher and host
*Paul Harvey	Commentator, host, and author
Gordon Hastings	Foundation executive
Paul Hedberg	Industry executive

Bob Henabery	Programmer and consultant
George Herman	News reporter, commentator, and writer
Robert Hilliard	Academic, author, and historian
Richard C. Hottelet	News reporter and commentator
Herbert Howard	Academic and industry expert
Charles Howell	Academic and archivist
Stanley Hubbard	Industry executive and satellite innovator
W.A. Kelly Huff	Academic and author
Phylis Johnson	Academic, author, and producer
*Casey Kasem	Entertainer and producer
Elihu Katz	Academic and author
John M. Kittross	Academic, author, and consultant
Steve Knoll	Freelance writer and journalist
Charles Laquidara	Deejay and performer
*Art Linkletter	Entertainer and producer
Robert Mahlman	Network executive
Leonard Maltin	Movie critic, author, and host
*Ed McMahon	Host, producer, and author
Larry Miller	Academic and deejay
Bruce Mims	Academic and author
Newton Minow	Former FCC Chairman and author
*Bruce Morrow	Entertainer and deejay
Robert Mounty	Network executive
*Arthur C. Nielsen Jr.	Audience research executive
Dick Orkin	Producer, writer, and voice artist
Peter Orlik	Academic and author
*Gary Owens	Entertainer, host, and voice artist
Tim Powell	Programmer and performer
*Ward Quaal	Industry executive and consultant
John Randolph	Actor and performer
Yuri Rasovsky	Producer and writer
Elliot Reid	Actor and narrator
Sam Sauls	Academic and author

*Daniel Schorr	Commentator, news reporter, and writer
Bobby Seale	Founder of the Black Panther Party
Ed Shane	Consultant and author
Allen Shaw	Network and industry executive
William Siemering	Cofounder of National Public Radio and consultant
*Howard K. Smith	News anchor, commentator, and writer
George Sosson	Industry executive
*Susan Stamberg	News reporter, producer, and writer
*Frank Stanton	Network pioneer and executive
*Bob Steele	Deejay and host
Christopher Sterling	Academic, author, and editor
Dusty Street	Industry professional
Sheldon Swartz	Archivist and deejay
Frank Tavares	Academic and industry expert
Marlin Taylor	Industry executive and programmer
*Studs Terkel	Author and entertainer
McHenry Tichenor	Industry executive
*Les Tremayne	Actor, host, and producer
Mary Ann Watson	Academic and author
Peter Wolf	Recording artist, performer, and programmer
Rick Wright	Academic and industry expert

Part I

The War Ends and the Picture Begins

1

The Quiet After and Before

Radio's Victory and Short Peace

Of the horizon to the zenith's height,
The locks of the approaching storm.
—Percy Bysshe Shelley

Radio was king of the hill in 1946. It had been the country's top form of home entertainment for nearly a quarter of a century, and it looked pretty certain that this would remain the case during the next quarter-century as well. In fact, things were looking pretty good on all fronts of the great American dream in the year following World War II. With victory's trophy in one hand and a laurel branch in the other, Americans believed the good life lay ahead for the taking, and it seemed inevitable that radio would serve as a central element in this rosy future. Few anticipated that the magic medium, as it was referred to with equal amounts of awe and affection, would soon face a life-altering, if not life-threatening, crisis.

David Sarnoff's proclamation at the New York World's Fair seven years earlier that the age of television had arrived did little to inspire concern that radio would soon be in any kind of jeopardy of losing its lofty status as living room centerpiece—or altar. In fact, in distinct counterpoint, the CBS network broadcast a play the same year by dramatist Norman Corwin, called Seems Radio Is Here to Stay, *that made an equally strong pronouncement of its own, one that was heard in millions of homes unequipped with a "picture" machine.*

The years between 1939 and 1946 found radio at the apogee of its value and popularity in U.S. society. The war had been good for the medium. Its credibility among listeners had ascended to new heights as it became the first place to go for news and information about the battle-fronts. It also continued to serve in the escapist role it had perfected during the Depression. The airwaves were rich with programs intended to take the listener away from the grim realities of global conflict.

Crowning the eventful decade was the Federal Communications Commission's action designed to guarantee that the public broadcast spectrum would remain a place where justice and equanimity would reside. The Fairness Doctrine—the "jewel in the tiara of public serv-ice," as one commissioner enthusiastically called it—was implemented in 1949. It seemed a fitting finale to one of the most robust eras in radio's service to the country and the world.

What follows is a discussion concerning the state of the audio me-dium as the nation prepared to enter a phase of unparalleled prosperity and the new age of "sightradio"—television. Throughout the book, each chapter's conversation is prefaced by the author and followed by the comments and observations of contributors.

Charles Howell: The end of World War II saw radio reach its zenith. The positive role played by radio during the war as a disseminator of serious wartime information as well as entertainment for the weary war worker boosted its stock with both the government and the public. Audio-equipment manufacturers had grown rich on government con-tracts, and, as the result of a tax loophole, the medium itself had been permitted to write off the cost of so-called goodwill or brand advertis-ing. Although this windfall seemed close to being eliminated by those concerned with "war profiteering," the government ultimately realized it needed radio's help more than it needed the money to be gained from closing the loophole. This money, which would have been sub-ject to excess-profit taxation, fattened the coffers of network radio nearly to the bulging point.

Irving Fang: Indeed, the radio industry emerged from World War II stronger than ever. CBS and NBC radio shows dominated the broad-cast entertainment business. The news departments plus the news com-mentators of ABC and Mutual were the sources of news and opinion for millions of Americans trying to cope during strange and uncertain times. Entertainment provided an escape from a world that seemed no less dangerous after the war than it did during wartime. At CBS William Paley spent the money needed to raid NBC of its top show-business talent. Meanwhile the manufacturing sectors were busy retooling to turn out the radios that people had been unable to buy during wartime. Now, unlike the Depression years, average folk had money in their pockets to buy receivers, which they considered not luxury items but rather necessities. In fact, one set in the parlor was no longer enough in many homes. Kitchens needed radios, too, especially when commentators talked during dinnertime. With factories preparing for peacetime, assembly lines poured forth an immense variety of goods. Because customers had the cash to purchase these products, advertisers filled the radio airwaves with tuneful sales jingles and spoken messages. Life was good.

Bruce Mims: Favorable economic conditions emerged at the conclusion of the war. Amid the prosperity, the Federal Communications Commission authorized the construction of many new, small-market, daytime-only stations. This enabled AM to evolve into a more localized communication service. Development of FM, which had been curtailed during the war, languished, although there would be a rush for licenses. As the forties drew to a close, the introduction of network television broadcasting portended the demise of network radio, but in the years immediately following the war, this was not an all-consuming concern.

Stanley Hubbard: The years following the war were good ones for radio. It was still at its peak, and there were radio stations in each large city and a few in smaller towns. As Bruce notes, this period marked the beginning of the opening up of the radio spectrum by the FCC. What I mean by that is the power of the big stations was diluted by the manner in which the commission allocated licenses for new stations. For example, back in 1945, here in Minneapolis/St. Paul where I live, there were only six or seven radio stations. Our station, KSTP, was the big NBC affiliate. WCCO was the CBS affiliate. These two stations dominated the market, much as the NBC and CBS television stations did at the beginning of the TV era. The other stations in town were WTCN, WDGY, WLOL, and WMIN. In many ways radio was like television today with the big network stations and then the independents. It obviously was a good time for established radio outlets.

Robert Mounty: Stan is right. Things were very solid for radio stations after the war. The atmosphere was quite positive, and there was continued growth that would last for a few more years.

Marvin Bensman: Certainly the FCC was intent on fostering the growth of the medium, especially in areas previously neglected. After the war, the commission took two actions that had a striking effect on the radio industry. First, it reduced the required minimum distance between two stations on the same AM frequency and, at the same time, authorized construction of daytime-only AM stations on frequencies formerly largely reserved for use of "clear-channel" or fifty-thousand-watt AM stations. Second, it opened a substantial band of frequencies for FM, or frequency-modulation, broadcasting—and implied strongly that there was a probability that within a few years all radio broadcasting would be shifted to FM. The result was a tremendous increase in the number of both FM and AM stations. The number of AM stations increased from approximately 940 in December 1945 to nearly 2400 in autumn 1952. In addition, FM stations, of which only half a dozen operated on an experimental basis in 1945, increased to approximately 650 in autumn 1952. At the same time, power increases were granted to many AM stations—increases that had been impossible during the freeze on equipment during the war. Some 650 to 700 stations were authorized to operate as daytimers. Things were moving.

LeRoy Bannerman: Nineteen forty-six and 1947 were profitable years for network radio. So it was decided that radio earnings should finance the development of television. By network officials it was deemed good strategy, for such sums could be considered business losses and as such partially absorbed as a tax write-off. Nobody realized that the radio networks were indeed financing their own burial.

John Kittross: Interestingly, despite the prosperity enjoyed by radio, the number of listeners actually went down during the years immediately following the war. The radio networks still reigned, however. They controlled the medium's programming schedule. There was tremendous growth in the sheer number of radio stations. Of course, this increased competition to a new level. Many prominent programmers, such as Storer, McLendon, and Storz, spent a great deal of time thinking about how to counter the networks' dominance. This led to format specialization and formula radio and the emergence of local radio.

True Boardman: In 1947, the bottom line still governed management's behavior in radio. The average station failed to provide enough cultural and educational programs. Profit was at the core of this deficiency. Actually, back then the networks provided far better public-service schedules than did local stations. Of course, many of these public-service programs were aired at poor times; that is, in time slots with few listeners. Of concern to me at the time was the fact that the radio networks programmed more and more shows containing violence. There was an overemphasis on evil doings and foul deeds in programs. You know, as I recall, there wasn't a whole lot of freedom of speech either. The bosses kept those with opinions off the air. Liberal voices were being lost to the air. There was not a lot of balance. The conservatives controlled the microphones even back then. Within a year or two of the war's end, I recall thinking that television would be a problem for radio and that those financially flush AM broadcasters should not be given first stab at the new TV frequencies or, for that matter, the new FM frequencies. I genuinely feared a monopoly of the airwaves, and I abhorred such a notion. It was my hope that more educational facilities would be born as a result of the new broadcast services. At the time, I was also concerned with what seemed the growing ineffectualness of the FCC. I believed that it simply was not working enough on behalf of the people. Far too many licenses were being granted, renewed, or transferred, and an abundance of evidence showed that the public interest had not been served. Back then it seemed to me a good argument that public-service radio was becoming less public and less service oriented.

Newton Minow: I'm not sure I concur with True. During those pre-television years, I think radio was much more socially important than it is today and much more attuned to the obligations of public service. I think the medium was working hard at being a solid citizen as the specter of TV closed in.

Ed McMahon: Yes, in my view, radio was working hard to meet its public-service agenda. The medium was enjoying its golden reverie, having been so vital in reporting World War II and its aftermath. There was a lot of good radio back then.

Art Linkletter: Ed is right, I believe. Surely in comparison to what it does today, radio focused in a very positive way on home and family. Good people imparting solid American values dominated the radio landscape after the war. *Ozzie and Harriet* and *House Party,* fairly typical of the programs offered, were quite popular.

Peter Orlik: It was a fruitful time in many areas of audio technology, too. For instance, the clumsy seventy-eight-rpm disk was replaced, as was the wire recorder. The postwar years brought improved recording techniques that had actually been a product of wartime research. This led to the loosening of the network bans on transcribed programs, thereby increasing production options. To provide an example, in 1947 Bing Crosby was able to convince ABC to record his show on the new magnetic audio tape and, in doing so, eliminate the need for him to replicate his performance live for western time zones.

Robert Hilliard: There was much to feel good about in radio after the war. Even as late as 1947, when radio was well into its third decade, there was still flexibility for the newcomer. That's when I started in radio. Having returned from service in the war, I was considering my college education and had decided that I wanted to be a writer. My professional work as a newspaper sportswriter and editor segued into playwriting and, stimulated by the work of Archibald McLeish, Norman Corwin, Arch Oboler, and others, I decided to try my hand in radio. I went to new radio station WTUX in Wilmington, Delaware (I was attending the University of Delaware at the time) and asked the station manager if there were any writing jobs available. "No," he said, "but I like your voice. Would you like to be our weekend morning man?" "I have no experience," I answered. "I don't even know how to work a control board." He said, "Don't worry, we'll teach you." So I became an announcer, a disc jockey, and a board operator and created commercials and handled traffic. I even had a chance to write, creating some of my own shows. I got the job with no experience, no sample tape, no audition, and no college courses in radio (few schools were offering a radio curriculum then), and I had never been in a radio studio or control room before. Compare that with what young people with degrees in broadcasting have to go through to get a job in radio today, and you'll understand what I mean about radio still being flexible as late as 1947.

Ward Quaal: Flexible it was. Things were on a pretty stable footing right after the war. Doors were open for many of the returning G.I.s as the medium continued to expand. Only a handful of radio stations were anticipating what lay ahead for them. Some began modest adjustments in view of the stirrings of television, but on the whole, it seemed a bucolic, if not somewhat complacent, time.

James Fletcher: Bucolic perhaps, but the five-year period following the war was a time of noteworthy change and foreshadowing. Three events were particularly important from my perspective. (1) The so-called *Blue Book* was created and, though never adopted by the FCC, had a tremendous influence on programming standards for several decades; (2) network television's first year of promising operation, 1948, marked the beginning of the death of the golden age of radio and a search for new possibilities; (3) the Liberty Network received attention from the entire radio industry, and that was important. The alternative modes of operation that this network championed included practices that spread quickly to other radio operations. I'm talking about the re-creation of sporting events and the use of popular-music recordings as a principal source of programming. Radio went a different way after the war.

Sign-off:

Write if you get work . . . hang by your thumbs.
                                        —Bob and Ray (WHDH-AM, 1947)

2

Assault of the Infant

Television Takes Over the Living Room

> *Radio is dead!*
> —Robert Sarnoff

Radio's future began to look a lot less bright at the beginning of the first full post-World War II decade as "radiovision" (an ironic early moniker for television) cast its spell on the American public. The audience for "affiliate" radio was decreasing, as were its revenues (dropping by $31 million annually between 1948 and 1952), further prompting the networks to shift their attention to the TV side of the ledger.

Talent raids conducted by the television networks were pillaging the audio medium of its stars and programs. William Paley's CBS network scored the biggest strike as radio luminaries such as Jack Benny, Red Skelton, George Burns and Gracie Allen, and Groucho Marx abandoned rival NBC.

In 1953, half the homes in the United States had a television set, and the radio receiver was exiled to less prominent locations to make room for it. Notes writer Ben Fong-Torres, "In living room after living room, families were carting in this long-legged invention called television and pushing the console radio out of the center of their evening lives."[1]

In 1946 there were about 10 thousand television sets in the country. This figure changed at an astounding pace. In his account of the era, CBS executive Sig Michelson reported:

> *There was only a handful more than 3 million television homes in the entire United States as the decade of the 1950s opened; when it ended,*

*the count had grown to more than 45 million, an increase of nearly
fifteen times. There were television receivers in approximately 9 percent
of American homes in 1950, in more than 86 percent in 1960.[2]*

*By the early 1950s, network radio was, for all intents and purposes,
a moribund programming service. Commented humorist Henry Morgan regarding the dreary situation, "Radio took a dive in 1951. . . . It
was gone!"*

*Within a few short years the medium scarcely resembled its former
glorious self. "The theater of the mind," quipped one acerbic media
critic, "has become TV for the blind." In his recent book,* Raised on
Radio, *Gerald Nachman observed, "Radio as theater vanished as
swiftly and as totally as had silent films before it, for a similar but
reverse reason: sound killed silent movies, and television finished off
radio."[3]*

Jack Brown: Radio was declared dead in 1950. True! One day in May
1950, the ratings (I think it was the Hoopers) showed that more people
had watched television the previous evening than had listened to radio.
A newspaper said it was "the beginning of the end" for radio. The
president of NBC commented, "I can see no future for radio." Most
people agreed that radio was dead. Radio was my career at the time, and
I asked a senior broadcaster if he believed that. He told me that in his
grandfather's day everyone had horses. Then, he said, along came the
automobile. Horses didn't disappear, he observed, but they just weren't
so important anymore. I thought that was a pretty glum outlook.

Ed McMahon: When television came along, all of the prognosticators
were sounding the death knell of radio. The dark clouds moved in
pretty quickly.

Gordon Hastings: Those clouds brought thunder with them. TV exploded onto the scene. It came so quickly that it left the radio industry
reeling. Radio was stripped of its stars and programming. I suppose the
upside to this is that it forced the medium to reinvent itself down the
line.

True Boardman: In the late 1940s, television was the invader at the
gate—the proverbial bad wolf knocking at the door. It started taking

over the living room. Up to then, radio was the ruling monarch. It was the nation's great pastime. Despite this, I remember feeling that radio would continue to reign for another decade or so before television took over, because right after the war there were more dramatic programs on radio than ever before. Maybe I was just being overly optimistic or hopeful.

Howard K. Smith: You know, I believe what stung the most was the fact that television, to a considerable degree, displaced radio's power. I think that news on radio had converted America from being isolationistic to being internationalistic. However, by the time another great issue arose—the civil rights movement—television had taken over. People witnessed these horrible events in Birmingham and elsewhere on the TV at dinnertime every night, and they became thoroughly disgusted and insisted that civil rights legislation be passed. By that time, television had really displaced the role and prestige of radio.

Les Tremayne: After a few years, there was little regard for radio. It just faded away for the most part as the industry put all of its efforts and nickels into publicizing the new visual medium. Parenthetically, if you watch TV today, it is guilty of the same flaws that radio had so often been accused of. All of this electronic entertainment has turned out to be a hungry maw. There are just as many soap operas and game shows as there were back then, and adding to this are those silly homemade videos consisting of weird and tasteless antics. So things have hardly improved.

Susan Stamberg: Television really elbowed radio out of contention as a home entertainment medium. Once radio devotees, many of us went to our neighbor's house to watch Milton Berle and Sid Caesar. I suppose "radiovision" was an inevitability. Radio itself knew this, too.

Dick Fatherley: By 1949 there were scores of defections to television not only by radio fans but by the medium's management and marketing veterans, writers and production people, and talent and technicians.

Stan Freberg: That's no exaggeration. Television put a lot of people out of work. The art of radio was put on permanent hiatus, too, when TV came along. The environment that had been so nurturing for the

Norman Corwins and Stan Frebergs was ruined. It was vanquished by the dull blue flickering light. You know, I did the last network radio comedy show in America. It was all gone before many people noticed it. The sponsors headed to TV, so the curtain came down on the kind of radio that Fred Allen and I did.

Irving Fang: David Sarnoff of RCA was pushing television hard, convinced of its potential market. As the decade of the nineteen-forties reached its end, a flight from radio to television began. Performers, writers, directors, engineers, and sales people were moving to the new medium. Money and enthusiasm were shifting also. Radio station owners snapped up licenses for the video medium. Despite the FCC-imposed freeze on new TV license applications, predictions were made of the demise of radio. However, like the news of Mark Twain's death, the predictions were premature.

Daniel Schorr: Premature, perhaps, but the advent of television was regarded by network executives as a prime threat to the audio service, because it would siphon away available advertising dollars and would lure away listeners.

Lynne Gross: Maybe the most significant victim in this transition was radio-network profits. The great prosperity that radio had enjoyed was pretty quickly followed by the loss of its economic base to television.

Christopher Sterling: The inception of the network television service swiftly threatened network radio's highly profitable reign, certainly during prime time and then eventually across the entire program schedule.

Daniel Schorr: I can recall a lunch in Paris in 1953—attended by CBS President Frank Stanton, David Schoenbrun, and Blair Clark—during which Stanton told us that the CBS radio network would probably not last more than five years.

Marvin Bensman: By 1952, CBS and NBC were serving from one hundred eighty to two hundred AM stations each; ABC had approximately three hundred seventy-five affiliates; Mutual had nearly four hundred. Trends continued, but during this period television became the dominant mass medium. Radio became less secure but actually grew in the number of smaller stations.

LeRoy Bannerman: As television flourished, it instantly became radio's arch nemesis, and there ensued a struggle within the networks for purpose and survival. A paranoia over program ratings bred the popularity of the giveaway shows—programs that awarded consumer products, all-expense-paid vacations, even money, to participating listeners and studio contestants. Radio was desperately doing whatever it could to offset the assault.

Frank Tavares: It is difficult to fully measure the impact of television. Suffice it to say it was formidable. As television became more popular and more affordable, radio programmers struggled to slow the defection of their listeners. But the young television networks made matters worse by mercilessly pillaging their radio neighbors of their program formats and personalities. Historically it could be no different. Every new communication medium subsumes the content and material of the one it replaces.

Dick Fatherley: I think the most significant loss to television was the relationship of hundreds of radio stations to their respective networks and vice-versa. As network television gathered momentum and strength, network radio grew increasingly weaker. According to a 1958 report issued by sales representatives Adam Young Incorporated, the top-rated radio stations in the nation's top twenty-five markets up to 1952 had been network affiliates. By 1957, the top-rated radio stations in 21 of the top 25 markets were independents, that is, nonaffiliates.

Bernarr Cooper: From my perspective, the most profound thing lost to TV was the imagination. Radio brought a kind of drama that existed only in the mind. That's what radio was about and TV isn't—the mind. Our imagination was forfeited with the introduction of, and ultimate domination by, TV. We had nothing to think about anymore. Everything was thought for us. It was just given to us with TV. No thinking was necessary with TV viewing. After television came along, we pretty much forgot about this quality of radio.

Marty Halperin: Bernarr has it right. You lost the wonderful "theater of the mind" with television. It was no longer there.

Dick Orkin: The other major loss was personal intimacy with the listener on a national and local level—that one-on-one sense that I am talking just to you. This shift also changed advertising's tone, content, and style. Instead of advertising being intimate and intrusive, it just became intrusive—make that annoyingly intrusive.

Larry Gelbart: I think the two things that were lost to television were subtlety and innocence. These were elements indigenous to creative radio during its reign, and they were vanquished by the arrival and subsequent dominance of the tube. Television marked the loss of the living room as the center of the American household.

Elihu Katz: I believe that television released (or superseded) radio as the medium of national integration. Thus radio became the medium of segmentation that divides and subdivides in order to serve every possible demographic, taste, and ideological group. Television also liberated radio from doing long-form programs. The same thing is about to happen to television.

Leonard Maltin: As has been mentioned, the rise of television had a curious effect on the quality of radio programming in the early 1950s. On the one hand, the exciting upstart medium drained a lot of talent from the radio pool. But at the same time, the people who stayed behind—writers, directors, actors, producers—found themselves with a new degree of freedom, since they no longer "mattered" as much. The result is that network radio shows from the medium's twilight years are in many cases extraordinarily good; they represent the work of the top pros in the business working at the peak of their powers. *Gunsmoke* would be just one example. Other shows like *Escape, Suspense, X Minus One, Dragnet,* and *The Halls of Ivy,* to name just a few, bear this out.

Walter Cronkite: You know, I believe the immediate impact of television was too subtle for most people to appreciate. There were those in radio, that is to say, most of my associates in radio, who never thought that this thing with pictures would ever take the place of radio. Now we're talking about radio news here rather than entertainment. They thought of television as an entertainment-only medium. They did not conceive of it as possessing the ability to cover news, the kind of actuality that would be necessary to make news programming on television possible. As a result they did not understand the impact that it was going to have.

Karl Haas: Radio has, indeed, suffered with the presence of television, but it has continued to exist regardless. Radio is by no means dead, despite all the predictions that it would be rendered lifeless by the picture set. It just became something else, perhaps not as marvelous as it once was, but it is still a very valuable medium in our lives, and we're lucky it stuck around.

Notes

1. Ben Fong-Torres, *The Hits Just Keep On Coming* (San Francisco: Miller Freeman Books, 1998), p. 15.
2. Sig Michelson, *The Decade that Shaped Television* (Westport, CT: Praeger, 1998), p. xvi.
3. Gerald Nachman, *Raised on Radio* (New York: Pantheon Books, 1998), p. 6.

Station jingle:

Keep listening and driving wherever
you happen to be
Just driving and listening
to KEWB.

3

Together . . . but Separate

When the Two Worked as One

Never again so much together.
—Louis MacNeice

During the infant days of television's existence, there was a level of exchange, if not camaraderie, between it and its senior cousin—radio—which was to become uncharacteristic of the relationship in the years to follow. At the onset, radio tolerated and even lent a helping hand to the rookie medium, despite the attention it was attracting. It was not an uncommon practice for television to simulcast radio programming. In fact, Lowell Thomas's evening newscast over NBC radio was repeated over the network's television airwaves. Upon the death of Ray Forrest, considered television's first personality, the New York Times *reported, "For months [NBC Television] employed no announcers, recruiting them from . . . [its] radio staff."[1] This spirit of cooperation carried over into the areas of sports and entertainment as well as news programming. For many radio professionals of the day, television was still more of an experiment than a bona fide competitor or threat, so why not behave graciously toward it? It would not last . . . would it?*

By the mid-1950s, network radio and television operated quite apart from one another—with only occasional collaborations (usually born more out of necessity than a genuine desire to "team up"). Ultimately this growing gulf served as a primary incentive for the audio medium to redefine itself in a way that gave it a new and distinct identity and life.

Norman Corwin: Shortly before the end of the war, CBS television was confined to a few suites in the Grand Central Station building. Of course, radio was the big player then, as there were but a handful (maybe a few thousand) TV sets in use. Well, the fledgling television medium took its cues, as well as program material, from radio from its inception. One such example was Gilbert Seldes's adaptation of my radio drama, *Untitled.* He literally presented it in its original form to the viewing audience. Later on, when the divorce between radio and television was all but final, CBS presented *A Plot to Overthrow Christmas* as a telecast of a radio show. A mock radio control room was constructed and a slave camera was put on me while I directed the action. The first half hour of the telecast consisted of our rehearsing the play and the second half hour was the telecast of our actually performing the script as we had originally done over CBS radio. I suppose it was inevitable that there would be an exchange of talent and resources. After all, radio's cupboards were plenty full, while TV's were quite barren, perhaps in more ways than one.

Richard C. Hottelet: There was some friendly borrowing from one another at the start. Although great radio genres, like drama, eventually disappeared when TV came on the scene, television certainly benefited from their existence. They inspired television to create some fresh and new things on its own. Radio was a solid role model for it. Actually, perhaps in part because of what radio had done, there was some good live-TV drama. Radio likely had an influence on the television work of Rod Serling and Paddy Chayefsky. TV election coverage also drew from what radio did.

George Herman: There was some cross-pollination during the transition phase when things went from radio to television. It wasn't as if there was this DMZ or unbridgeable gulf back then. For instance, consider the political conventions in Philadelphia in 1948. CBS had put up an enormous radio newsroom and office off to one side, plus a booth overlooking the hall (similar to the usual radio booth). The TV anchor (in the studio) was Douglas Edwards, who broadcast the CBS evening TV news on WCBS-TV in New York. I was Doug's radio writer, putting together his seven forty-five A.M., fifteen-minute local radio presentation, but I was working general assignment at the conventions. They were my first, and I soon became confused. The tickers' bulletin bells would ring and the radio stars—Ed Murrow and others—would read the bulletins, which often contained something to the effect that the state of so-and-so had caucused and the vote cast was twenty-three-and-one-third votes for Harry Truman and the rest for Strom Thurmond, or whomever. The stars and analysts would nod and say, "Oh, that's very important!" and I realized I didn't know why. So I commandeered a small looseleaf notebook from supply and wrote down the names of the forty-eight states and the territories and how many votes they each had. Then, after a few minutes of going through the bulletins, I copied down all the results, and soon I had the whole count of caucuses on two facing pages and could add them in my head. About then, Henry Cassirer, head of the television operation, burst into the newsroom and asked the radio guys how many votes Truman had. Murrow replied, "A lot!" The newsroom editor added, "A commanding lead!" And the senior convention editor offered, "Almost unbeatable!" To which Cassirer replied, "That doesn't help me. This is TV. I can't use adjectives. I have to show a picture with numbers." "Okay," said the editor, "give me twenty minutes and I'll go through the copy and add it up for you." Lee Otis responded, "You don't have to do that. I've got all the numbers right here." "Herman," said Cassirer, "you got a jacket?" "Yeah," I said. "Put it on," he said, and pushed my necktie up to the collar. He then walked me over to the door and gave me a shove through it, and all of a sudden I was on television with Doug. On cue, I stumbled through the numbers for the viewing audience. I was quickly detached from radio and reassigned to TV in order to help keep their count up to date. I had learned something during all this; TV wouldn't or couldn't use fancy words and phrases. It needed to show the hard visual facts—graphic readouts. Yet radio was still the big medium. CBS-TV had only about half a dozen stations back then and a very small audience.

Don Godfrey: In many respects, radio helped make television possible. In fact, one of the most overlooked contributions radio made to U.S. electronic media is television. We've all heard about how television took away radio's golden-age programming. What we don't hear about is the fact that on a local level it was generally a radio station that financed a television start-up operation. Industry and business patterns, established with the historical evolution of radio, were superimposed on the new television medium. Radio has made some very significant contributions to television and other media-industry operations. It helped break new ground in many new media endeavors.

Marty Halperin: Skilled and talented radio people were there for television to draw on, and, likewise, television provided many radio people with a place to ply some of their skills and learn a bunch of new ones. Admittedly, there was more to be learned than to apply in television, but still there was some place to go. TV mostly took when it came to programming, but occasionally it worked in reverse. For example, *Have Gun Will Travel* debuted on television and then found a place on radio too.

Larry Gelbart: Many radio writers were recruited by television, and the results were not always pretty. The first writing I did for TV was on Easter in 1950. I was one of the writers on Bob Hope's staff, responsible for his radio scripts and his personal appearances and for "punching up" his movies. His TV debut was ours too. The first "spectacular" we wrote for him was spectacularly bad. What we wrote were essentially radio jokes that required him to be dressed in silly costumes and wield comic props. Hope's TV shows down through the decades changed little. Although I wrote for TV and radio for the next two years, I learned nothing about writing for television until I left his employ.

Daniel Schorr: In the end, I think that television aided radio news. Correspondents became primarily TV correspondents, doing radio reports as a sideline. But in this way, television news effectively subsidized radio news. It wasn't just a one-way street with TV taking everything, as is the common notion.

Charles Howell: There were performers who effectively worked in both media and, in doing so, benefited both. Arthur Godfrey is a good example of this. No figure really signifies the transition period more vividly than he does, I believe. While a success in television, Godfrey, perhaps more than any other figure, helped move radio from the network-oriented era to the format era in effect today. His show, *Arthur Godfrey and His Friends,* was a hit simultaneously on television and radio.

George Herman: Like many partnerships, this one did not last either. In 1950, I was assigned to cover the Korean War and found that the radio- and TV-news divisions had split apart and were jealously competing with each other. We had no TV crew in Korea. We bought film from Telenews, and there was no TV reporter per se. Finally, CBS-TV sent over a single, inexperienced crew, but we radio people were repeatedly ordered to have nothing to do with the TV-news operation. They had no office staff, no permits, and even their cables (including one peremptorily ordering the camera crew to "at once stop doing business with Herman") could reach them only through me. I finally wrote a letter to CBS in New York offering to hire the TV operation its own staff and rent another office for them and help them get permits, but noted that it all sounded foolish and expensive to me and why couldn't we unite the two news divisions, at least in this overseas war coverage operation. Finally the two divisions were united and did work together. However, for the most part, we radio people concentrated on the story, meaning the tactics and the strategy of the allied effort, and the crew concentrated on the battle pictures, usually with no correspondent narrating from the field, only from New York. When the war was over and I was assigned to cover the White House, replacing Charles Collingwood in 1954, it was for radio only, and Charles Von Fremd continued as the CBS-TV White House correspondent. We were good friends and worked closely together. Eventually, the CBS radio- and television-news divisions reunited. When I returned to the White House to cover JFK, it was for both. I had already covered the 1956 Adlai Stevenson campaign for radio and television.

Ed McMahon: There was a point around this time when radio and television worked in unison, or sort of combined forces. There was an exchange, a back and forth of talent. NBC provided worldwide coverage with *Monitor,* and I was one of the hosts. Local radio was everywhere, in every town, and TV was really just kicking in, so it sometimes needed an assist from the radio side.

Les Tremayne: During this period, there was work in both TV and radio for those of us who had worked pretty exclusively in radio. We could do commercials and narrations. Those who couldn't make the transition went into real estate or other businesses. When TV became so dominant, radio was permitted to simulcast its broadcasts. That, I suppose, was around the time the fortunes of radio were down and those of television were headed skyward. The two mediums were together . . . but growing quite separate.

Note

1. Robert Thomas Jr., "Ray Forrest Is Dead at 83," *New York Times,* March 21, 1999, p. 31.

Sign-off:

And that's the top of the news as it looks from here.
—Fulton Lewis, Jr.

4

The *Word* Is the Thing

The Substance of Sound

> *All is not sweet, all is not sound*
> —Ben Jonson

What radio's writers and performers had engendered during the medium's less-than-three-decade "golden" run was quite extraordinary indeed. Bearing testimony to this fact today are hundreds of audio tapes featuring some of the outstanding work of heyday practitioners. Moreover, in most cases, one need only visit the local public library to find volumes of published verse and prose radio plays by Norman Corwin, Archibald MacLeish, Stephen Vincent Benet, Pearl S. Buck, Arch Oboler, W.H. Auden, Arthur Miller, and a host of other radiowrights (a term coined by Corwin).

Over the years, several attempts have been made to revive the art form, but few have met with lasting success. In 1998, veteran radio producer Himan Brown brought drama back to network radio, but it was short-lived, prompting the octogenarian to seek airtime on public radio.

Corwin's indictment in 1950 that the medium had become "a trade outlet, not an art" was reflected in Brown's own lament nearly a half century later that commercial radio has little to do with intelligence and creativity. (For an example of the "word" as it was brilliantly employed for the radio audience by one of the medium's true masters, turn to chapter 24.)

True Boardman: It is too bad that television did sweep in, because radio drama had really come of age and was on the verge of evolving into an even greater art form. One can only imagine what magnificent radio plays would have been written had the art form been permitted a continued existence on the networks. At the time, my thinking was that the very nature of the video medium would mean the dramatist's work would demand the kind of attention that radio seldom received, and that would mean that for drama to be effective it would have to be better. That would also mean that as writers we would simply have to work harder. Back then I had a theory concerning television. I believed that it represented the completion of the full cycle in the history of drama. That, of course, was an optimistic view, but the view I held at the time.

Bernarr Cooper: Radio drama was perhaps the medium's greatest gift to our culture. It was radio's most significant contribution to the world. It was an original art form, perfected by great experimenters like Norman Corwin. There was some very special work being done, but not after TV came along. It disappeared after that.

Erik Barnouw: That it was a great medium for the writer became all the more obvious to me when one day during the war I received a phone call from a representative of Pearl Buck, who had just won the Nobel Prize for literature. I was asked if I would meet with Miss Buck for lunch. I couldn't imagine why she would want to meet with me. But we did meet and after we ate she said, "I would like to register for your course in radio writing." I said I would be delighted and asked her why. "Well, I've been asked by the State Department," she said, "to write some radio programs to be beamed by short-wave to China." Then she said, "And I wonder if it would be possible to avoid a fuss being made over me when I come to Columbia." She was probably the most famous writer in the world at that time, and everybody did make a fuss over her wherever she went. I suggested that she might register under her husband's name and that I would get someone to go through the registration line for her; I asked my mother to do the registering and she did, enjoying the little deception as she signed up Pearl Buck for the course as Mrs. R. Walsh. I wondered whether Pearl Buck would actually show up for class, but at the very last moment in she came with a hat pulled down over her eyes, and she took a seat in the back of the room. I also wondered whether she was actually going to participate in the class; she turned out to be one of the most avid students I have ever had. She was very meticulous and never missed a deadline for any assignments I gave. She later wrote the radio series that had prompted her to come to my class. Six plays, under the general title *America Speaks to China,* were translated into Chinese by an Office of War specialist and short-waved to China.

Studs Terkel: The importance of the "word" was lost when television took over the living rooms of America. Sure, there were plenty of trivial programs on radio at the time, but there were also brilliance and creativity that have never been equaled by television. For example, Dylan Thomas's "Under Milk Wood" was far more potent and stirring on radio than it was when it was brought to television. The use of the imagination amplified its beauty. It was the word in glorious flight. There were never couch potatoes in radio, only television. TV feeds the viewer everything. There is no need to engage the mind. Radio piqued the imagination. It was far more challenging and full of discovery. The wonderful word was lost when television ambled in.

John Dunning: I believe (and I'm using this line, at least in the working draft, in a novel I'm writing) that radio was the ideal partner of the printed word. It's a perfect medium for the short-story dramatization, for the slice of life that makes its point so well in twenty-nine minutes and thirty seconds. There is no white space anymore. The pregnant pause is a thing of the quaint and half-forgotten past. Today they have a gizmo built into the audio equipment that creates noise if there's more than a couple of seconds of silence. Picture this, a true account of my attempt to play an old *Dragnet* on KHOW in Denver. As the script goes, Sargeants Romero and Friday are talking in the wake of a tragedy. Anyone who is remotely familiar with Jack Webb's work knows how well he used those great pauses. Here's how it's supposed to play:

> ROMERO: Well, Joe . . . what's it all prove?
> *(Brief pause as Friday mulls it over)*
> FRIDAY: You don't give a kid a gun for Christmas.

Here's how it sounded on KHOW:

ROMERO: Well, Joe . . . *swisssshhhh!* . . . what's it all prove? *swisssshhhh!*
FRIDAY: You don't give a kid a gun for Christmas.

Ed Murrow wouldn't stand a chance today, what with computers kicking mindless noise into all those gaps he always left. "This . . . *swisssshhhh!* . . . is London!" Doesn't have quite the same bite, does it? Today they insist that you get all the call letters in constantly. I remember when I was at KNUS, one of the out-of-town consultants got the staff together and said the call letters were mandatory every three minutes. I raised my hand and said, "That's going to be difficult on my show. I do old-time radio, and my shows are programmed in blocks of thirty minutes. I never let them be interrupted or cut." Without batting an eye the consultant said, "Maybe we could create some kind of subliminal sound bed that would kick in and say 'KNUS Denver' throughout your tape." Everyone laughed except me and the consultant. I took him absolutely seriously, and I gave him one of those looks that kill and said, "Don't even think about it." You've got to be something of an SOB yourself if you want to protect your program. It helps, too, if you're not in radio for your living.

Sam Dann: We can get scholarly about this and delve for abstruse explanations, but one fact cannot be denied. Television is a passive experience. Radio required the listener's cooperation. Radio supplied the words, but the listeners created the picture. Radio disappeared, except for some heroic efforts made by Hi Brown, who continues to fight the good fight. One of the reasons for this disappearance is that we have become an impatient country with practically no attention span. We want immediate answers and instant gratification. We don't have the time for leisurely and reflective listening anymore. It takes effort to listen.

Steve Knoll: As David Brinkley pointed out when he delivered the Elmer Davis Memorial Lecture at Columbia University in 1966, "Radio was quite different. People listened to what was said and how it was said."

Howard K. Smith: With radio's displacement, we lost some of the respect for words or the expression by words. In early TV, there was a great respect for words from the time of radio, since so many people had their roots in the older medium when it was predominant. A lot of that was lost when television took over. The imagination was much less stimulated after the arrival of television. The viewer just doesn't have to participate and think as he or she did when tuning in radio. For example, you don't encounter anything as evocative as Norman Corwin's marvelous prose poem, "On a Note of Triumph."

Larry Gelbart: When I was writing for radio, I was a tadpole. It was writing for the medium that taught me how to write for the stage and for the screen. Radio taught me that words have to stand on their own. America is, in fact, suffering a word famine. In what others have described as a postliterate world, we hear nothing at all that has been thought out, weighed, or fashioned by people with the experience to do so. A thoughtful play on Broadway is a rarity. Musicals reign. Lyrics, the libretto, both take a back seat to special effects and/or spectacle. As for movies, increasingly it is the director's, not the writer's, vision that reaches the screen. So, to me, at least, words are not what they once were. A case in point: The movie *Titanic,* which won Oscars for everything from stem to stern, did not receive a nomination for best screenplay. Doesn't that also say something about how little we expect from literature in any of the media these days? Was the work of radio's best writers "literature?" Corwin's was, without a doubt—absolutely. I'm not really familiar with Benet and Auden's radio work, but it is hard to imagine that anything they wrote for any medium wouldn't fall into this category. Oboler? Literature of the potboiler variety, I would say (being extremely careful not to tumble off my high horse).

Marty Halperin: Hal Kanter is quoted as saying (but he steadfastly denies it) that "[r]adio is the theater of the mind, and television is the theater of the mindless." And that is probably true.

Himan Brown: Besides radio dramas created by the likes of Norman Corwin, there were some marvelously written series, which were an important part of evening listening. You know, many of the afternoon soaps were written with considerable deftness, too, and should be given some due notice.

Stan Freberg: Occasionally, in the years following the takeover by television, I have been allowed to flex my creative wings for radio. My maraschino cherry spot for the Radio Advertising Bureau in the 1960s, wherein I drain Lake Michigan and convert it into a huge dessert, demonstrated, for those who had forgotten or never knew, what a splendid medium of the imagination radio could be. You know, that radio script inspired a couple of writers some years later. Stephen King and David Mamet cited it in their books on writing (*Danse Macabre* and *Writing in Restaurants,* respectively) as evidence of the power of the carefully chosen word on the imagination. Of course, neither got the piece right, but I was flattered to be noted as an influence just the same. A lot of writers who had penned for the audio medium, for people like Jack Benny and others, found employment in television. Many of these former radio writers had to remind themselves to avoid too much description, that is, with sound effects and other devices. It wasn't necessary when the audience could see everything. So for some, the transition was challenging. Benny, for example, would forget this. There would be a door knock and Benny would say on television "Oh, there's somebody at the door. I'll just walk over to the door here (walk, walk, walk) and open the door." Then suddenly these people realized, "Hey, the audience can see him walking across the room!" They had written for a medium without pictures for so long—actually there were great pictures in radio, but they existed in the minds of the listeners—that they had to remind themselves that the audience could now see what was happening.

Elliott Reid: Of course, words and radio are synonymous with Norman Corwin. His pen enriched the radio canon. I can safely assert that one event that played a primary role in the evolution of radio was the work of that gentleman. In my opinion, he was the first writer to bring true intelligence, wit, and top-drawer quality to the medium. Even today he is still at it. He always treated actors with more warmth, affection, and respect than any other director I've ever worked for. He is a man of mammoth talent and humanity.

Frank Stanton: Elliott is right. Norman Corwin's work was extraordinary. His sensitive, literate style provided listeners with lines they would long remember.

Norman Corwin: If I had to title what I'm about to say, I'd call it "Dead for a Ducat." As he draws his sword to kill the snitch hiding behind an arras in the Queen's chamber, Hamlet cries, "Dead! For a ducat, dead." Substitute commercial broadcasters for Hamlet, and old-time radio for Polonius, and you have what happened to America's senior electronic medium. Having developed its own literature, radio was generating a new breed of dramatists and poets, even a new art form, when television arrived. The overlords of broadcasting quickly learned that by unloading audio stations and concentrating on video, they could vastly increase the flow of ducats, so without ceremony they promptly scuttled radio. "Killed it," as John Dunning says more economically elsewhere in these pages. Despite its flaws, radio was not in the business of granulating news, fragmenting the attention span, insinuating sex into commercials, shelling out billions to bring mass football to the hearth, and persistently drawing down epithets equivalent to "couch potato" and "boob tube." In its brief fling as sovereign of electronic communication, radio enjoyed occasional states of élan unlike anything experienced by its successor. This may seem a rash claim until one asks how many times television attracted anything like the following published encomia in response to various radio broadcasts: "heady power . . . wonderfully perceptive . . . in a category of its own making . . . historic impact . . . inimitable . . . soaring majesty . . . stirs the soul and brings tears of joy . . . a vast announcement . . . a terrific interrogatory . . . one of the all-time great American poems . . . rich diversity . . . should takes its place in the halls of fame . . . embodies hopes and lessons, entreaties and thanks . . . merits a repeat from every pulpit in the land . . . epic . . . held the hearts and minds of the American public as nothing done before or since . . . gripped the attention and chilled the marrow . . . opened and closed a war, dedicated a parliament of nations, provided an ode to lay presidents to rest." This is not to say that TV was and is without champions and triumphs of its own. It gave us Dave Garroway, Fred Coe, Ernie Kovacs, Rod Serling, Paddy Chayefsky, John Frankenheimer, Horton Foote, Sid Caesar, Cliff Norton, Delbert Mann, Reginald

Rose, Norman Lear, and a good many other candidates for lasting fame. It produced winners seriatim, like *All in the Family, I Love Lucy, Sunday Morning, Nova, 60 Minutes, Roots, The Simpsons, Masterpiece Theatre,* and *The Civil War.* Its coverage of transcendent news events has often been first-rate. But when it comes to the propagation of a distinct literature, to presenting drama that excites the imagination and engages the mind, to accommodating poetry through the kind of creative imagery and enlightened language routinely rejected by television, in all these exercises radio is still the vehicle of choice—a vehicle, alas, that for the past fifty years has either made only local stops or has not run at all. In its cultural heyday radio was an educational force, capable of implementing valuable curricula such as those of *The American School of the Air.* It promoted programs like *Invitation to Learning;* carried symphony concerts without commercial interruption; employed Arturo Toscanini to conduct a network's house orchestra for several seasons; invited major poets to read and discuss their work; attracted writers of rank, including Dylan Thomas, W.H. Auden, Stephen Vincent Benét, Maxwell Anderson, Robert E. Sherwood, Carl Sandburg, Norman Rosten, and especially Archibald MacLeish, to write expressly for it. Not only did MacLeish deliver two landmark scripts *(Air Raid* and *Fall of the City),* but he was among the first to define and articulate the properties of serious radio writing, differences that set it apart from writing for stage, television, and films—principles that made radio a friendly country for stateless poets:

> A radio play consists of words and word equivalents and nothing else . . . there is only the word-excited imagination . . . a theater in which poets have always claimed peculiar rights. . . . Nothing exists save as the word creates it. . . . Over the radio verse has no visual presence to compete with. Only the ear is engaged, and the ear is already half poet. It believes at once: creates and believes.[1]

MacLeish clearly sounded a rallying call to bards whose tragedy is isolation from any audience vigorous enough to demand their strongest work. A fact that everyone knows and no one observes is that the technique of radio, the ordinary commercial technique, has developed tools that could not have been more perfectly adapted to the poet's uses had he developed them himself.

It is a waste of thought to hope that in the future, radio specials like *The Fall of the City* will be transmitted simultaneously over hundreds of stations, as was the case when it was first broadcast. There are not enough affiliated stations or unaffiliated ducats to bring that about, even though there is always more than enough green stuff floating around in corporate kitties to fund, say, a *Seinfeld* series for years on end, at a million dollars per episode to its star alone.

Note

1. Joseph Liss, *Radio's Best Plays* (New York: Greenberg, 1947).

Sign-off:

If the creek don't rise and the good lord is willing, we'll do it all again tomorrow.

—Charles Laquidara

5

In Mourning and Evening

"The Way It Was" Radio

The true paradises are paradises we have lost.
—Marcel Proust

As the years radiate swiftly by at the speed of sound and light, and radio's much revered golden-age fades even deeper into the long-ago, far-away past, the laments over its demise seem to grow louder and more melancholy, particularly by those who knew it first-hand and by those who helped create it. One wonders how it will be remembered when these aging citizens of the honeyed airwaves are no longer around to offer their living testimony of its greatness. As behavorist and ardent radio listener B.F. Skinner once wrote, "Education is what survives when what has been learnt has been forgotten." We are all a little bit better educated because of radio's salad days. Its myriad lessons will continue to enrich the ages, including those yet to be lived, if we keep our ears attuned and attentive.

For better or for worse, the radio plays and programs that have enjoyed the most renewed attention (modest though it be) over the years have typically been those possessing mainstream (pop culture— prosaic and trendy) qualities and characteristics—The Shadow, Inner Sanctum, Dick Tracy, The Lone Ranger. The heyday dramas and plays that embraced headier themes, as well as traditional and innovative literary devices and conceits, are rarely rebroadcast. They belong to a time when attention spans were longer than soundbite length.

True Boardman: It is a shame to have lost something so precious. I think most of us whose lives had been radio looked to television with a mixture of fear and hope. In the former case, we were anxious about losing what we had, and in the latter case, we were hoping that the new medium would provide us with opportunities for creative expression. It didn't quite turn out that way.

Frank Bresee: The painful fact is the medium's full development was cut short by television. Many historians agree that the years leading up to television saw radio reach nearly the summit of its powers. These were important years in the growth of radio; in its realizing its fullest potential. Not only did the networks broadcast thousands of programs, but with the advent of World War II, the American Forces Radio Service (AFRS) created and presented many of its own shows. These programs included *Command Performance, Mail Call,* and *G.I. Journal,* in addition to the rerecordings of most of the American network shows that were broadcast to the U.S. service personnel throughout the world. *Command Performance* was first broadcast on March 8, 1942, and was produced by the War Department. During its five years on the air it featured virtually every famous Hollywood artist including Bob Hope, Bing Crosby, Dinah Shore, Rudy Vallee, and George Burns and Gracie Allen, to name only a few. The show was written in answer to requests mailed in from servicemen all over the world. The stars appeared on the program for free and considered acting on *Command Performance* a small part of their contribution to the war effort. Probably the most famous *Command Performance* was broadcast on February 15, 1945, when an all-star cast was assembled at the Columbia Square studios of CBS in Hollywood for a radio spoof of the popular Dick Tracy newspaper comic strip. The show was titled *Dick Tracy in B-Flat or For Goodness Sake, Isn't He Ever Going to Marry Tess Truehart?* The cast featured Bing Crosby as Dick Tracy, Dinah Shore as Tess Truehart, and Jerry Colonna as the Chief of Police. The balance of the cast included Bob Hope as Flat Top, Cass Daley as Gravel Gertie, Frank Morgan as Vitamin Snowflake, the Andrews Sisters as the Summer Sisters, Frank Sinatra as Shakie, and announcer Harry Von Zell as old Judge Hooker. *Time* magazine described *Command Performance* as "the best wartime program on radio." Most of the big shows on radio kept the nation entertained during the dark days of World War II. Bob Hope and his band of gypsies traveled to army camps every Tuesday for his weekly NBC radio show, as did Kay

Kyser and his Kollege of Musical Knowledge, Coca-Cola's *Victory Parade of Spotlight Bands,* and *The Vaughn Monroe Show.* It was radio at its most vibrant.

Ed Shane: My father worked for the Georgia Railroad, an important link that shuttled wartime soldiers and medical supplies between Atlanta and Camp Gordon (later Fort Gordon) near Augusta, Georgia. Dad didn't see duty on the rails. He was an office worker. Like his colleagues, he was asked to stay "at home" during the war and keep the trains running. Mother didn't have to wait for his return from distant shores, thus the year's head start on the boomer bulge. The radio I remember was truly "theater of the mind." The clearest recollection I have of the era is Jack Benny's vault, deep in the cellar below his home. Still in my mind is the sound of the miserly Benny going down creaking stairs, being accosted by the guard, and slipping by alligators to get to his treasure. I see the pictures so vividly. Then I remind myself that the only visual reference I have to that period is a radiant gas heater in my parents' bedroom (where the radio was) and a large metal screen that kept a toddler from stumbling into the open gas flames. The radio created images that a little terrace apartment near Atlanta's Piedmont Park could not. The social aspects of radio were foreign to me. I knew that people listened to music and soap operas in the daytime and to dramas and comedies at night. That was about it. I can't tell you now which programs were my parents' favorites, nor do I have recollections of specific nights of the week when they made appointments with the radio for entertainment. My parents spent more time playing cards with friends and attending church functions than they did listening to radio. They had no car during the first ten years of my life so there was no car radio to attract them or influence me, which is what the radio did particularly well back then—attract and influence.

John Dunning: I suppose we still have radio, if you want to call it that. Certainly you'll locate no theater of the mind on the dial today. You can flip your switch and noise comes out, but you will search long and hard to find anything worth listening to. Today we endure entire formats, some of which last for years with no break in the gray conformity. Talking heads. Stations playing the same tired tunes from the same tired playlists, day after endless day, the same one hundred songs in a kind of hit parade from hell. Consultants flitting from city to city making sure it all sounds alike. To confirm this you only need to travel. Go to Cincinnati or Los Angeles and it sounds just like Denver. They even have the same silly catch-phrases. If it isn't "music and weather together," it's "traffic and weather on the tens" or some such nonsense. Jacor owns everything, and if they don't, it's because they have just sold out to an even bigger corporation that will continue homogenizing the air until we all begin to gag on it. Program directors all think alike—"You're only as good as your last book," they will say. This is a phrase you will hear from coast to coast. They all keep one eye on the ratings, but when numbers begin to fall, they never understand why. When TV killed radio, radio had to become something else. No longer could it be an after-dinner entertainment for hours at a stretch. Attention spans plummeted, drivetime became vital, soundbites came into vogue (though they wouldn't be called that for years), and the great march to grayness began. Is it any wonder we long for radio's former glorious self?

Marty Halperin: The loss of radio to TV was really the loss of the imagination. Now you've got a generation of people who have no idea of what radio was like. They don't know anything about body fades or off-stage voices. With TV, what you see is what you get—nothing more. There's no denying that TV brings the visual in all its beauty into the home, but where is the mental and creative stimulation you got in radio? In radio you could build such magnificent sets and scenery and great characterizations and characters all in the listener's mind, which you could never reproduce on the television. William Conrad, because of his bulk, could not make the transition to TV in *Gunsmoke*. He was not what people wanted to see, but he had been Matt Dillon before and as much as James Arness was on television.

Walter Cronkite: Indeed, a lot of great talent was lost to television. For instance, in the case of Norman Corwin, very much was lost to TV when it took over the American home. His words were simply beautiful to hear. He wrote for the ear better than possibly anybody in the business. Much of the same quality was lost in radio news. The ability to paint a picture with words as done by the best broadcasters was unique and very special. I'm thinking, of course, of Edward R. Murrow and the London coverage during the war as a prime example. The ability to communicate ideas has been lost almost entirely in television, it seems to me. The commentaries of Erik Sevareid, for instance, and Kaltenborn and others, were lost when we surrendered to the picture.

Richard C. Hottelet: Over the years, there have been a few short echoes of the old days, for instance on CBS Radio's *The World Tonight,* which picks up longer reports than is the custom in present-day radio news. These are a rarity, however. When it happens, I'm happily taken back to a uniquely different era in the medium's now considerable lifespan.

Gary Owens: While on the subject of being taken back, during a conversation with Orson Welles, I asked him about his radio persona. He wanted to give everything a dramatic flair, be it Shakespeare or Alfred Neuman [sic], and he told me that as a film director he was influenced by such great illustrators as Noel Sickles, who, along with Milton Caniff, gave him marvelous cartoon angles that he utilized in various media. At lunch in the nineteen-seventies, Welles told me he loved the work of Alex Toth. Orson created verbal images on radio as he did in his films. Of course, lest we forget, he frightened the country twice in one evening with his great powers: first with his *War of the Worlds* broadcast and then when the rotund genius read his grocery list on the air. Such superb radio directors as William L. Robson and Norman Corwin defined radio at its best. After learning by listening to the golden-age greats, I became a professional broadcaster at the age of sixteen. I started as a newscaster-announcer-sportscaster and then, by accident, I became a top-forty deejay. It was in Omaha. I was the news director at the time, and the early-morning deejay was angry with management. He quit in the middle of his show and stomped out of the studio, puffs of smoke expelling from his pores. The chief engineer and I were the only two in the station at six A.M., so I took over, despite the fact that I had never played records on a turntable before. I goofed many of the records, but my ad-libs about being nerdish and goofing up pleased the audience. Within a month, I became number one in the city, and it began a great career for me in the world of contemporary hit radio. So TV's climb rather paralleled my own.

Studs Terkel: The arrival of television was a horrendous thing for the medium of radio. It was devastating for the radio artists as well as the public. Television was a very poor replacement. Its content is all surface and no substance. The freedom that radio artists had was lost in television, which is a much more mechanical medium. Something truly significant was forfeited when radio was displaced by TV, thus forcing radio to reinvent itself into something not quite as good.

Norman Corwin: I personally have cause to mourn the passing of "the way it was" radio, because for over a decade in history's shortest golden age, I wrote, directed, and produced for CBS when its eye was wide open. I worked like hell and loved every minute of it, but when television began to glow in living rooms and radio was ditched, it felt to me and many of my colleagues as though we'd been equipped with marvelous horses to ride and had ridden them far and fast, and then suddenly they were shot out from under us.

Leonard Maltin: I think it's a shame that television and radio couldn't continue to coexist. The popularity of the radio shows in the 1950s proved there was still a strong listening constituency, but the real money was to be made in television, and it was certainly cheaper to fill airtime with a disc jockey spinning records than to contribute to the cost of original dramatic and comedy programming.

Sign-off:

And now, if you'll get close to your radio there, it's time for a goodbye kiss.

—Gary Owens

6

Reinventing Itself

A Winning Formula Is Found

> *Not till the hours of light return,*
> *All we have built do we discern.*
> —Matthew Arnold

The radio schedule was rich with offerings as the war came to its sober conclusion. Soap operas alone claimed seventy-five hours of network time each week. This was rivaled by comedies and dramas. Nearly a third of the network schedule was allocated to some form of live or recorded music. The top shows in 1948 included the trenchant gossip of Walter Winchell, the comic shenanigans of Jack Benny, and the gripping and evocative drama of the Lux Radio Theater. *In 1950, an enterprising young Scotsman by the name of Gordon McLendon was recreating baseball games for his affiliated stations. By now the transistor had been created and radio's mobility (inspiring such slogans as "radio—your constant companion") would soon be enhanced through miniaturization.*

As the first few years of the 1950s witnessed the spectacular rise in the popularity of television, radio set about the task of recreating itself through program specialization. The age of format radio was launched. Soon the deejay ruled the airwaves, and listeners were offered a wide variety of carefully designed music stations to tune. The hot industry buzzword of the new age of radio was "demographics." Stations targeted their programming to a specific segment of the listening public in order to attract advertisers seeking the same group of consumers.

This strategy, coupled with the new teen music craze—rock 'n' roll—and the contemporarily designed portable receivers flooding the market, saw radio regain its audience and profits, if not its former program aesthetic. By the late 1950s, more people tuned radio and more advertisers used radio than at any other time in its history.

Elliot Reid: When I was a child, growing up in a suburb of New York City called Pelham, you could leave your house, walk down the length of the street, and not miss a single word of *Amos 'n' Andy*. On radio today is there anything as universally tuned as that was? Still in its early days, radio was as widely accepted as TV is today and was, in fact, a godsend to people severely affected by the Depression—those who wanted entertainment but needed to save every penny. A movie had to be really special, and a Broadway show was out of the question! It cannot be overstressed that radio rescued us. Even children obligingly returned home from their street games in time to hear *Amos 'n' Andy*. Sometimes we had to turn off the radio for a while so the batteries could recharge and we'd be able to hear all the *Maurice Chevalier Show* or the *A&P Gypsies* (weekend offerings, if I recall correctly), and phone numbers were just four digits and you had to wait for the operator. In the very early days of radio, the choice of programs was meager. Children today are inundated with choices, and theme parks, and air conditioning, and comforts and diversions the likes of which we knew nothing of, nor even dreamt of, and yet we had many things that delighted us and made us happy, and as primitive as they might be viewed by today's kids, we were content. And we did have Playland in Rye, an excellent amusement park that was nirvana for us. Change is unavoidable and not always better than what it supersedes.

Gary Owens: Historically, after World War II most of the dramatic and adventure shows that had been the exclusive province of radio or film segued to television. *Gunsmoke* was an exception, of course, lasting many more years on radio with William Conrad playing Matt Dillon and Parley Baer playing Chester. The overview of radio since television arrived reveals the birth of national top forty in the fifties and sixties, the rise of album-oriented rock (AOR) in the seventies, and urban contemporary in the eighties. Top forty changed its moniker to contemporary hit radio (CHR). Middle of the road continued to thrive in hundreds of cities with the *Music of Your Life* syndicated approach as did other similar formats. Radio, indeed, may have changed from World War Junior, but it is healthier than ever in terms of profit. I've been in syndicated radio around the world since the early sixties, and the field gets better every day. Excuse me, I'm now going to give excerpts (former cerps) from my speech! "Ladies and Gentlemen and fellow microphones, . . ." Inventor and Nobel Prize winner Guglielmo Marconi certainly knew what he was doing. The father of wireless telegraphy transmitted the first transatlantic wireless signal in 1901. Before that he was going to the gym every day getting on the exercycle with a headset of two huge Morse-code telegraph machines on his ears! And then he found a way to transmit sound without wires. We had the same thing on *Laugh-In*. It was called Jo Ann Worley! He also invented a CD wrapper you can actually open. Yes, radio has had quite a metamorphosis (I believe it was the great radio entertainer Will Rogers who said "I never met a morph I didn't like!"). In the fifties radio turned from quiz shows, soaps and serials, comedies and dramas to DJ shows, à la top-forty style. It was a transmutation from sitting at home gawking into space and laughing while listening to Jack Benny to dancing around the room mouthing the words of Fats Domino and Elvis Presley.

Himan Brown: William Paley was quickly losing interest in radio as television came on the scene. Right after the war he scrubbed my *Green Valley* series. So I immediately tried to update its theme to dealing with postwar issues. Emerson Radio bought the series and we went on the air every Sunday afternoon before a live audience. We ran for almost another three years, then Emerson became very involved in television, which was really blossoming. Actually, a few of my other shows remained on the air a while longer. Television really didn't impact radio's audience until 1950. *Inner Sanctum* mysteries remained on the air until 1954 on Sunday nights. No more *Nero Wolfe, Bulldog Drummond,* or my kids' shows though. By 1950 the handwriting was on the wall. TV had taken over. But my persistence in keeping "audio" drama alive made it possible to sell NBC a morning series (1955–1959) called *Morning Matinee.* It featured Madeline Carroll, Celeste Holm, Don Ameche, Eddie Albert, and Lee Bowman. When the series went off the air in 1959, I had no more radio.

Frank Bresee: In an effort to save radio entertainment, the NBC network presented a Sunday-night, ninety-minute "live" spectacular with some of the brightest stars of Broadway, motion pictures, music recording, and radio. It featured comedy, music, and dramatic presentations, and it kept the country entertained. The program was titled *The Big Show* and was hosted by the legendary Tallulah Bankhead. Guests included Bob Hope, Ethel Merman, Jimmy Durante, Fanny Brice, Frankie Laine, Groucho Marx, Dean Martin and Jerry Lewis, and Fred Allen (he came out of retirement for the show and became a regular supporting-cast member). Meredith Wilson and his orchestra supplied original music for each show. *The Big Show* cost over ninety thousand dollars for each hour-and-a-half program and was well worth it. Some of the sponsors were RCA, Anacin, and Chesterfield cigarettes. *The Big Show* was on the air for over seventy-five weeks, and finally bowed out on April 20, 1952. But radio wasn't dead. *The Third Man,* starring Orson Welles, was broadcast in new episodes (as recorded by BBC in London). Syndicated programs, such as *Bold Venture* with Humphrey Bogart and Lauren Bacall, and the Alan Ladd program *Box 13,* continued to bring entertainment to listeners. Arthur Godfrey continued his radio show on CBS. It was heard every morning for ninety minutes. In fact, for a few years it was heard as a simulcast on CBS television. Actually, more people heard the show on radio than saw it on TV. At one time, Mr. Godfrey and his programs were responsible for more than twenty percent of all CBS revenues.

LeRoy Bannerman: To my mind, 1945 was the climactic year of radio's golden age. That era of innovative achievement emerged in the mid-thirties when the medium developed the technical proficiency to permit audio experimentation and program aestheticism. It made possible the origin of many classic programs—in drama, comedy, variety, the documentary—which were popular well into the decade of the fifties. But, as an evolutionary period, it is difficult to mark the precise beginning or the exact end of that era widely known as the golden age. A few programs came into existence during the late twenties and lasted until the early sixties. After television arrived, it was obvious radio's approach to broadcasting had to change.

Bernarr Cooper: After TV, radio became a completely different animal than it had been. It became much more of a background service, one that occasionally became foreground with news coverage. After the nineteen-fifties, radio was really not much more than a reminder medium. It was no longer the valuable commodity it used to be.

Dick Orkin: Eventually, or perhaps inevitably, radio, with the cooperation of the music industry, became a "jukebox" of pop music punctuated by contests and "time and temp." Of course, this occurred after radio abandoned its original programming model, which provided listeners with dramas, soaps, comedies, and variety shows. The medium was forced to devise replacement entertainment that was low budget, so local radio turned to popular music in a "participating" program setting.

Jack Brown: Radio did lose its soaps, its dramas, and its variety shows to television. But radio lived on. It changed. Rather than try to compete head to head with TV, it developed a new approach of its own. It had already tried a whole new concept in music programming. Instead of live orchestras and music from broadcast transcription services, stations began playing the popular records of the day. Hosts such as Martin Block in the East and Al Jarvis in the West built large followings. Disc jockeys proliferated. New music formats were developed.

Peter Orlik: The business model was being modified as well in radio. The change from "time franchises" to "spot advertising" on the network level began in 1945 when William Paley of CBS made a move to assert greater network control over the schedule and secure the production profits that had been going to advertising agencies' wholly owned shows. Paley set up CBS's first programming department to develop show concepts, especially comedies, that would then be offered to advertisers. By 1948, CBS had put thirty-six of its own initially unsponsored radio series on the air, many of which were great financial successes for the network. CBS now sold individual commercial minutes (spots) in the shows rather than turning over the entire program and its time period to an agency. The network thereby acquired greater control over shows rather than risking a lot of money on a single program sponsorship.

Douglas Gomery: Of course, TV was the catalyst for much of this activity. It had been just around the corner for most of the thirties, and if not for the diversion of industrial capacity to the war effort, the shakeup of network radio might have begun much sooner. As previously stated, the war had been responsible for the most lucrative years of network radio, despite the looming specter of television. When the war ended in 1945, the networks were ready to move ahead with television as soon as the industrial reconversion occurred. The infamous talent raids of 1948 were another sign of the times. William Paley showed top stars a method of avoiding the ninety-percent tax bracket by selling their programs as properties to his network. These stars formed the foundation of the network's television stable. A new arrival on the network radio scene, which for some time was indicative of the changes taking place in the medium, was the "giveaway" show. It was best exemplified by the first of its breed, *Stop the Music*. The idea was simple. Announcer Bert Parks would stop the band in mid-song and then place a call to somewhere in the United States. If someone answered the phone, was listening to the show, and could name the song, he or she would be buried in an avalanche of consumer goods, sometimes worth as much as thirty thousand dollars. In little more than a year this young program knocked the venerable veteran Fred Allen off the air and spawned a host of imitators. In the comedy arena, as stalwarts like Bob Hope and Jack Benny transferred their energy to television, newcomers like Bob Elliot and Ray Goulding *(Bob and Ray)* and Stan Freberg and his troupe of regulars (Dawes Butler and June Foray, most notably) gave radio comedy a more modern sound. Other shows of more than passing interest during the twilight of network radio included two adult science-fiction offerings, *X Minus One* and *Dimension X.* Adult science fiction was tailor-made for radio, and it seems odd that network radio was almost an afterthought by the time these programs aired—perhaps ten years too late to make the sort of impact they deserved to make. What we think of today as the network radio era didn't just suddenly end when Uncle Milty took to the home screen. It lingered through the nineteen-fifties and even into the nineteen-sixties, slowly losing its audience along the way.

Marvin Bensman: The same networks continued to provide service to radio stations in the years following the war. However, they actually did so with more affiliates. As Professor Gomery already mentioned, one major shift in network status took place shortly after the war. CBS, which for years had run second in popularity and in volume of business to NBC, simply bought a number of NBC's most popular entertainers—in particular, comedians—and placed their programs on the CBS schedules. The result was that CBS replaced NBC as the "leading" network, NBC was a very close second, ABC still a poor third, and MBS a very weak fourth. Also, during this period, a new coast-to-coast radio network came into being—the Liberty Broadcasting System, which started by providing recreated baseball broadcasts to some fifty stations and later expanded its activities until it provided a few hours—or in some cases, less than one hour—of program service daily to perhaps three hundred stations. Unfortunately, after approximately two years of operation, Liberty was forced into bankruptcy in 1950. As might be expected, the types of program provided by radio were greatly affected by the new economic conditions that were quickly unfolding. On the radio network programming front, several changes occurred. Evening variety programs decreased, evening music programs decreased even more significantly, as did evening quiz and audience-participation programs. News programs and evening talk programs held at about the same level. During the daytime, there was a striking increase in low-cost variety and in quiz and audience participation (combined, since it was often difficult to differentiate between the two forms). It is worth noting, too, that during this period, magnetic recorders were introduced and networks for the first time permitted the use of recorded music. But the really important change was in sponsorship of network programs. Whereas in 1944 and 1945, at least ninety percent of all radio network programs were sponsored, by 1951 not more than forty-five percent of all evening network hours and a smaller proportion of daytime hours had national sponsors. Possibly eight to ten percent of all network programs were "co-ops"—that is, fed to affiliated stations for local sponsorship; at least forty percent were broadcast on a sustaining (free) basis.

Lynne Gross: It is certainly true that the radio networks were busy recasting themselves. In fact, all of radio was trying to reinvent itself. Soon, with radio's close ties to music, came the rise of the superstar disk jockey, like Alan Freed, and the station programming innovator, like Todd Storz and Gordon McLendon, but the radio networks refused to be counted out of the picture.

Marvin Bensman: In the years since 1952, the type of programming provided by radio networks changed almost completely. As stated, networks lost their once-popular evening entertainment programs; most disappeared by 1956. Daytime programs lasted a few years longer, and the last radio soap operas went off the air in 1960. By this time the only conventional programs remaining were ABC's *Breakfast Club,* the *Arthur Godfrey Show* on CBS, and the news programs on the hour—five minutes in length. The *Breakfast Club* went off the air in 1968 and the *Arthur Godfrey Show* bit the dust in 1972. One network innovation that proved moderately successful was NBC's *Monitor,* which ceased to air in 1975. By 1960, radio networks were no long paying their affiliates for carrying their programs. The major emphasis was news.

LeRoy Bannerman: Local radio soon supplanted network radio, in that it could best provide programs and features of communal interest. With television, the public no longer needed the cosmopolitan, national appeal of network radio. They tuned in for local weather, local news, local advertisers, and music of regional taste. In short, radio became community oriented. Utilizing only a disc jockey, it was an economical approach to broadcasting.

Marvin Bensman: The increasing number of stations going on the air that could not find a network to affiliate with found that playing records, the lowest-cost programming, was what they could afford. By the late nineteen-fifties, probably some eighty to ninety percent of all radio stations were filling most of their program time with recorded music interrupted at intervals by short capsule news summaries. Stations began to specialize in various formats. Many of the top-forty stations tried to be different and attract listener attention by using a variety of gimmicks—special sound effects, station-ID jingles, giveaways, record hops, and contests. After 1958 a trend away from the dominance of top forty became evident. Specialization became more sought after as the elusive radio audience was wooed.

John Kittross: I'd provide a thumbnail sketch of the nineteen-fifties this way: There is a huge move to TV by talent—both creative and managerial. The radio networks die. The amount of radio listening drops. Unit concepts of "drivetime," and so forth, are implemented. Top-forty formula radio takes hold. FM grows very slowly, while there is growth in the amount of AM automobile reception. TV use keeps on growing in the home.

Peter Orlik: In 1954, television advertising sales first surpassed those for radio, and network-scripted entertainment programs accelerated their exodus to where the money was. This caused more and more airtime to be filled locally with more modular "deejay"-type programs. Appreciating this fact, NBC president Sylvester "Pat" Weaver brought the *Monitor* concept to the network weekends. A potpourri of interesting modules strung together from eight A.M. Saturday until midnight on Sunday, *Monitor* was the archetype of the new network radio. It served both listener-lifestyle and affiliate-scheduling needs by providing a wealth of easily digestible segments designed to enhance a variety of listener and local-station use patterns that capitalized on the medium's portability. The end of this period saw the final conversion of network radio into a purely supplemental service for local stations. On November 25, 1960, the last four long-running soap operas (all CBS properties) left the air for good. *Young Dr. Malone, Right to Happiness, The Second Mrs. Burton,* and *Ma Perkins* wound up their plot lines and faded away as their sponsors abandoned them for the greener pastures of video soaps.

Frank Tavares: Radio programming had certainly changed, as had the audience and the way people listened. Radio's audience had always been largest in the evenings, when listener leisure was the greatest and AM signals traveled the farthest. During the forties and fifties, when commercial radio networks were the strongest, it was pretty easy to demonstrate the popularity of network radio programming. This is when the icons of the medium and the tales of shared cultural experience were born—theaters delayed performances until after certain shows were broadcast, folks listened to their favorite programs waft from open windows during strolls along neighborhood streets. As we know, when the programming and audience went to television, the radio networks' strength quickly dissipated, eventually fading away, except for hourly news broadcasts. Several important points should be made about the older medium as it adapted to the demands of the younger. First, radio programming in the early nineteen-fifties evolved rapidly. The dominance of network programming gave way to local origination, and the type of programming presented to the listening public changed. As more programming—with the exception of national newscasts—originated locally, specific radio formats developed. Stations strove to differentiate themselves from one another. Second, audience usage evolved rapidly. Morning and drivetime became the peak listening times instead of the evening. Third, advertisers were asking new questions of radio broadcasters, not just about the numbers of listeners, but about *who* was listening. Demographics started to define the differences among different radio stations as much as the programming.

Bud Connell: Frank's right on all three counts. Let me pick up on his programming point. Early masters of the radio medium wielded their strongest influences through creativity merged with the manipulation of various format factors. The early formatics used consisted of music, news, information and public service, personalities, promotion, and, of course, commercials. All elements were carefully scheduled, but the almighty commercial was the supreme entity to which most media masters bowed. The new local programming delivered massive audiences and a lower cost per thousand to the advertisers. Through the years, commercials were the building blocks of great broadcast fortunes. Conversely, when programmed to excess, they turned audiences away and were the poison leading to financial death for the deserving greedy. Commercials continued to supply smart radio operators with high-octane fuel. The more money (fuel) the media masters accumulated, the more cleverly and expertly they manipulated the other programming factors. Each format factor or element influenced the success or failure of all radio entities and, as a by-product, created unintended changes in our social and cultural fabric. Of foremost consideration when designing a sound were type of music, selection, and rotation schemes; quality and frequency of news, or lack of it; recurrence of services such as time, temperature, and weather; caliber and stature of talent and patter; timeliness, cleverness, enjoining addiction of promotions, and so on. There were minor things and there were major things to weigh in putting together a viable format. It was not a simple puzzle.

Marvin Bensman: Moving along on the programming clock, in April 1965, a New York station became "all news." Still others developed into "all talk," and some stations experimented with bringing back old radio dramas. Finally, specialization reached what seemed an all-time high when in December 1965, an "all classified ad" station was authorized in California. It died shortly thereafter. The early nineteen-sixties for local radio programming was a period of development and experimentation. Many changes in regulation and competition affected the industry during this period. Radio recovered from the shock of television. More AM and AM-FM combinations reported profits. FM began to move as AM became overcrowded.

Marlin Taylor: As we rolled into the nineteen-sixties, radio entered another innovative era with the introduction of new music formats. We at WDVR, "Easy 101," launched what became the highly successful beautiful-music/easy-listening format, which over the next ten years swept into virtually every market in the nation and became such a favorite that the majority of stations airing it reached the upper heights in the Arbitron ratings. The easy-listening/beautiful-music format reached its peak of popularity in the nineteen-seventies, bringing joy to millions of listeners, many of whom remained tuned from sunrise to bedtime. For this format we created a long list of musical selections that became major favorites with our listeners.

Marvin Bensman: As the nineteen-seventies approached, a lot of format experimentation was going on. For example, "underground" stations played off-beat records and longer album cuts, black and ethnic stations grew in number, automated and prepackaged music stations sprang up, and the cross-over of music into less well defined categories created some programming ambiguity. The small market stations continued to provide a block-type format with different types of material presented at times when the audience was available.

Bruce Mims: In the late nineteen-seventies, the film *Saturday Night Fever* ignited interest in disco music. Certain major market stations enjoyed spectacular ratings after adopting it as a format. A similar phenomenon occurred in the country format when *Urban Cowboy* hit the movie screens. The success of the film propelled many artists of the genre into the mainstream popular music spotlight and numerous singles crossed over from *Billboard*'s "Country" chart to its "Hot one hundred" list.

Peter Orlik: Looking backward for a moment, perhaps most significant in the nineteen-sixties, certainly in terms of network radio, is ABC Radio's 1967 decision to split itself into four separate networks to better serve the supplementary needs of diversely programmed affiliates. This really completed network radio's conversion to a servant of local outlets. In putting together this new design, ABC Radio's president, Ralph Beaudin, adroitly avoided violating the FCC's chain broadcasting rules by making certain that the four new nets were transmitted at different times of the day rather than simultaneously.

Robert Mahlman: Not until January 1968, when ABC began that bold venture into four demographically programmed networks, each with separate on-air news and sports people, did network radio change and finally come to the obvious conclusion that stations throughout the country were targeting specific audiences. The question might be asked, given that radio networks were losing millions at the time, why didn't they just go out of business? One significant reason was the climate at the FCC. There was a mindset in Washington that the radio networks, despite operating at a loss, provided an important national service and "the high profits made from owning TV stations and a TV network could easily be used to maintain the radio networks' loss." Also, prior to ABC's changes in 1968, all of the networks utilized their high-profile TV personalities and TV news bureaus to minimize network radio losses as much as possible. It took ABC's four networks until 1972 to break even. Whether the venture was born by pure necessity or was a concept that was long overdue is not clear, but there was a decision to go forward with a full commitment by ABC's top management. ABC built the most up-to-date facility in the world, located on Broadway and Sixty-First Street—away from the headquarters at 1330 Sixth Avenue. Tom O'Brien, a veteran newsperson at local New York stations, staffed the network facilities and bureau with radio people. He pioneered the "voice actuality"—teaching newspeople to get the voice of the person making news (with a tape recorder) rather than a newsperson telling the story. It was a revolutionary concept at the time. This is how the four new ABC radio news networks broke down: contemporary (for stations targeting demos—listeners— under twenty-five), information (for stations targeting adults aged twenty-five to fifty-four who still wanted a large amount of news and sports), entertainment (demos aged twenty-five to fifty-four not wanting as much programming as provided by the information network), and the FM network. The FM network was geared to "good-music" or "beautiful-music" FM stations, since FM took until almost the mid-nineteen-seventies to expand into other formats. ABC's FM network went from seven affiliates to over 197 in less than a year under the genius of Alex Smallens, director of the network (his father was a famous conductor of the Berlin Symphony and the Radio Music Hall Orchestra).) The FM network changed its demo approach in the mid-nineteen-seventies as FM discovered its music appeal to the under-thirty crowd. The pioneers of the new network radio demographic concept, Wally Schwartz, Ed McLaughlin, Tom O'Brien, Ralph Beaudin, Dwight Case, and others gave network radio a badly needed new beginning. It was fourth down and goal to go with everything to gain or lose when ABC scored first.

Marvin Bensman: It is really hard to overstate the significance of ABC's move to split into four distinct network services. A key factor in the proposal was that it allowed ABC to affiliate with four stations in the same market. The FCC approved, and the policy was polished with Mutual offering an exclusive black network and NBC trying an all-news network, which lasted for less than a year.

Ed Shane: The raw experimentation that heated the city parks and streets and the rock palaces in the sixties tempered the seventies, becoming the cool control of Bob Seger or the frosty detachment of Steely Dan. Radio did the same, organizing itself into systems like the "superstars" format, in stark contrast to freeform styles that dominated FM just a few years earlier. The slick rhythms of disco smoothed the edges of what once were "race" and "soul" music and created a new style of "safe" pop radio.

Stan Freberg: Well, for me, seventies radio had mainly disintegrated into rock music deejays and an occasional five-minute newscast. Very pat and very predictable. Boring (SFX: snore).

John Kittross: If I may interject another thumbnail sketch of the period after 1971. Due to transistors, integrated circuits, and boom boxes radio is everywhere. AM has become talk radio, and FM became music radio. Classical music pretty much disappeared. Lots of "wallpaper" radio. Public radio takes off and garners listeners. The radio medium is completely deregulated. Local radio exists only during times of crisis.

Marvin Bensman: There were plenty of changes on the network radio front in the eighties and plenty of evidence that they were still players. Westwood One bought both NBC Radio and Mutual Radio. GE repurchased RCA. At the time, NBC had over seven hundred fifty affiliates and Mutual had seven hundred thirty-one affiliates. CBS had three hundred sixty-six, and the National Black Network had nearly one hundred. ABC was purchase by Capitol Cities. There were also AP and UPI Network News and the Sheridan Broadcasting Network with its one hundred seventeen affiliates. Rounding things out was the United Stations Network with over one thousand affiliates. There was a host of other smaller services in operation as well.

Newton Minow: You know, during the seventies and eighties there was a deterioration of the medium caused in great part by what had become excessive competition.

Dick Fatherley: Maybe it is excessive competition. I don't know. I do know that there has been a substantial drop in the cultural levels of most noninformation radio programming available to the listening public. That would include the feigned erudition of noncommercial radio entities like NPR's *All Things Considered,* which cannot and does not consider "all" things. The repetition of rap recordings on radio about killing police officers, its other vulgarities and antisocial chants, the demagoguery of Limbaugh, and the prurient self-interest of Howard Stern and Don Imus bear witness to the vacuity of the nation's top radio programmers. The medium is in a tailspin because of their inept decisions. Their apologists call it "hip" programming. Their defenders say it's "protected" speech under the First Amendment. And the beat(ing) goes on.

Dick Orkin: Tastes seem to have fallen to an all-time low in radio. According to the people who keep track of it, there are some forty-three different radio formats available, most of them having to do with music and talk. Yet radio has the same dull, repetitive, and cloned sound everywhere you go. The vocal sounds, the phrasing, the slogans, the formatting routine, the music and talk—all the same! To paraphrase a writer for a Detroit newspaper, "You can travel the width and breadth of the U.S. and encounter one cloned cliché after another." He further observed that the way it's going he wouldn't be surprised that one day we just get one dull and predictable-sounding radio station coast to coast. I agree.

Walter Cronkite: Radio remains a cultural influence. Certainly in the music it plays. Even there, I'm afraid, the good music stations are few and far between. As for those of us who appreciate traditionally good music, well, we really have very few places to go on the dial. That's just the way it is now, it seems.

Deejay patter:

Ahh-Bay! Unh! Ahh-Bay! Koo Wee Summa Summa! Yowsah-Yowsah!
—Murray the K.

Part II

The Second Coming of Radio

7

Home of the Hits

Going to the Top 40

Come on, and go, go, go . . . !
—Cousin Brucie

Top 40 may justifiably be called the "cool" granddaddy of all music radio programming genres, because formula radio itself was actually born during its inception. The seeds of all-hit radio had been planted while the medium was still the darling of the American living room. Midway through the Depression, the concept of spinning the popular songs of the day for listeners was introduced by Al Jarvis on the west coast and Martin Block on the east coast. The program these enterprising young broadcasters—these first "deejays"—conceived was Make Believe Ballroom.

Another twenty years passed before radio, now in a battle for its very survival, offered an updated version of the Jarvis/Block approach in the form of top 40. A whole generation of radio entrepreneurs helped launch the most popular youth-oriented music format of radio's "second coming."

Other legendary programmers, like Bill Drake, Gerald Bartell, Chuck Blore, Bill Gavin, Mike Joseph, Rick Sklar, and Buzz Bennett, brought their special touch to top 40 and in doing so strengthened its amazing hold on the hearts, if not the minds, of the nation's teen and young-adult population for generations to come.

Over the years, top 40 has been reinvented and/or retooled many times in order to retain or regain its appeal and relevance to its listening audience. The rapid evolution and resulting permutations in rock

*and pop music have made it difficult at times for the format to main-
tain a clear and steady course. Nonetheless, it has never been out of
the ranks of the ratings winners for very long.*

Christopher Sterling: The rise of formula or top-forty radio music
formats was instrumental in saving the medium after the networks
died. The format also set the pace for the growth in suburban radio
stations.

Sam Sauls: In 1955, rock 'n' roll found radio with the help of people
like Alan Freed. Formula radio, the place where rock located a home,
was first launched in the guise of top forty. Todd Storz, Gordon
McLendon, and several others got it going. Later, it would be refined
by Bill Drake and some of his contemporaries.

Bud Connell: Radio as we know it today began with the spaced repetition of hit records. Todd Storz, a young man barely in his late twenties,
started the rapid transition from New York-Chicago-Los Angeles-based
network programming to local hometown programming soon after he
and his father acquired KOWH in Omaha, Nebraska, in 1949. The
young Storz was a ham radio operator and accustomed to being in
control. In the very early fifties, music and news became Todd's principal output at his radio outlet. Warm and fuzzy on-air personalities and
primitive listener promotions coupled with the primordial popular-music programming and the nation's first hourly newscast garnered immediate dominant audiences. Storz required that the station be identified
before and after every record. He also involved the audience with contests and promotions and in the creation of news with the original
"Newstip of the Week" award. The ratings steadily increased until little
daytimer KOWH was the most highly rated radio station in the nation.
In spring 1953, Todd's newly acquired WTIX in New Orleans coined
the term "top forty." Radio, which had been ground down to near
extinction from 1948 to 1952 by television's massive assault on America's free time, began its rapid rocket ride to recovery. In 1956, Todd
Storz called me from Hot Springs, Arkansas, while I happened to be
reading an article in *Time* about his breathing new life into the radio
medium. I studied his picture as he spoke. He didn't look much older
than me, but his image in the magazine made him appear like a giant to
me. He was calling to invite me to join KOWH, and I was thrilled. The

next twelve years would be my own rapid rocket ride into top-forty programming and management.

Casey Kasem: Around the mid-nineteen-fifites, Todd Storz owned TS Broadcasting. Among others, he had two employees: Les Stein (aka ABC-TV talk-show host Les Crane) and John Barrett (KRLA general manager, who hired me as a deejay in 1963). Storz had just bought a station in New Orleans. He sent Stein and Barrett down there to listen to all the local stations in order to decide what format to use in the area. But, as Stein and Barrett learned to their amazement, the highest-rated station around was a little out-of-the-way outlet that played top-ten local hits every afternoon. That's all they did for about an hour, but they had the highest ratings! Stein and Barrett reported this fact back to Storz, who directed his New Orleans outlet to do the same thing—play the local top-ten hit songs over and over again. It worked. They then expanded the playlist to twenty and then to forty. Meanwhile, in Dallas, Gordon McLendon, who had started out as an on-air talent, ended up owning stations like KLIF. At the time, his forte was recreating baseball games on the air for local fans. I had done the same thing over the P.A. system in my high school days back in Detroit, but I recreated only the last minute or so of the game, not the whole game like McLendon. He'd do play-by-play as results came over the wire service. He would add sound effects, and there you would have it—live baseball coverage. He picked up on the top-forty thing pretty quickly, too. Between Storz and McLendon, the top-forty schematic began spreading across the country. At WJBK in Detroit, where I was working as a disc jockey, we created our own variation—playing the top-forty-five hottest hits in the Motor City. We called it "formula forty-five," and our introductory promos rang out: "Coming to Detroit—Formula forty-five!" The trouble was no one out there knew what it meant. Some listeners thought we were advertising a cough medicine. I got the notion of doing a national top-forty countdown show back in my high-school days in the late nineteen-forties.

Shel Swartz: From my perspective, people look back at the so-called golden age of radio through rose-colored glasses. The truth is, there was some horrible programming, especially at the network level. The networks dominated programming back then to the degree that it really inhibited creativity on the local level. All the local announcer had to do was drop in an ID between network feeds. In fact, in the early days of the networks, they even had their own announcer ID the local affiliates. Top-forty pioneer Todd Storz realized the ho-hum nature of much of what the networks were offering and dropped a lot of the network feeds on his station (KOWH), opting for local origination.

Dave Archard: In late 1958 I was employed at WALT 1110 AM in Tampa as a deejay. I was in seventh heaven because we played Sinatra, Tormé, the Four Freshmen, Basie, Kenton, and others. We had loyal listeners at nearby MacDill Air Force Base, but nowhere else. Management had to do something to build an audience. WALT's general manager at the time, George Fee, heard of two stations in Orlando—WLOF and WHOO—that were tearing up the market by playing a restricted list of songs as determined by *Billboard* and *Cashbox* magazines. With WALT program director Bob Walters in tow, Fee made a trip to Orlando. It resulted in the hiring of the young programming genius at WHOO, Roy Nilson. Nilson soon arrived with some cardboard boxes full of records and tapes. "There's your new station," he told us. At the time, the leading stations in Tampa-St. Pete were WSUN, still airing ABC's *Breakfast Club*; WDAE, with the CBS Arthur Godfrey/soap opera blocks; and WFLA, featuring a half hour women's show that offered recipes each morning. Record artists in "deejay slots" consisted of Perry Como, Patti Page, Eddie Fisher, and so on. On a sunny day in December 1958, Nilson had us play Sheb Wooley's "Purple People Eater" over and over with no commercials, promos, or news—just the legal ID at the top of the hour. The resulting phone calls blew out a circuit in our section of downtown Tampa. A city policeman stopped in to ask if everything was all right. The excitement had begun. The next day, "New WALT Radio" hit the air with a "modern radio" format. This was before cart machines were available. All spots, jingles, "pick hit" intros, and so on were cut on discs! In the control room, we deejays ran our own board with four turntables constantly spinning. Audience reaction was immediate. The other stations rubbed their ears in amazement as we hammered home the station's moniker—"New WALT Radio!"

Gordon Hastings: Summing it up, I'd say radio's new era was brought about by the coincidental emergence of rock 'n' roll onto the American music scene and the development of inexpensive, portable

AM radios. While the audience for dramatic programming had vanished, the industry quickly seized the opportunity to become the country's primary mass purveyor of the popular new music.

Dick Clark: For years, music was promoted by song pluggers in retail outlets. It then moved to promotion people talking to orchestra leaders. Inevitably, radio became the most important source for the promotion of popular music. Through the thirties, forties, fifties, sixties, seventies, eighties, up until today, radio has been the engine pulling the music train behind it. Aside from being a source of inexpensive programming, music on radio became a key marketing tool for record companies.

Gordon Hastings: A more personal kind of relationship between the station and its listeners developed through the use of audience-involving contests and promotions. The formatted radio station, with its stars on disc, replaced the old network program format. New local radio personalities were born out of this environment. I believe that rock music saved the day for radio, especially during this very uncertain time, by keeping it connected to a mass audience.

Dave Archard: Looking back, the music chart consisted of a weird mix of white rock 'n' rollers (Frankie Avalon, Freddie Cannon), black artists (Fats Domino, Clyde McPhatter), and country singers (Faron Young, Jim Reeves). Years later, separate music formats were broken out as other stations scrambled to imitate the top-forty style. Our format called for us to play the number-one song on the New WALT Radio top-forty chart every hour on the hour. At the time, that song was Ray Charles' "What I Say"—complete with a loud and long drum solo.

Douglas Gomery: The format that Storz and McLendon helped create was the first highly codified music-radio programming approach. Most of the formats that followed it were patterned after it in one way or another. In his book *The Development of Top 40 Radio,* David T. MacFarland cites the following hallmarks of the format:

- Strict adherence to a programming "clock hour" called for certain elements (news, weather, songs) to occur at very carefully prescribed times

- Programming concerns took precedence over sales
- Disc jockeys controlled the playlist
- Target audience music preferences had primacy over management's tastes
- There was heavy use of promotions and giveaways
- There was increased call-letter repetition using highly polished jingles

By the nineteen-sixties, as top forty proliferated, stations added new wrinkles, but playing the best-selling hits remained the format's principle goal.

Ed Shane: Top forty played music designed uniquely for the youth market. This kind of new radio became essential to our lives. When rock 'n' roll burst onto the scene and top-forty radio was invented, every kid in America was sure that it had been done as a personal favor. The prudish, the safe, and the square were put aside. In their place was a new culture that our parents hated, so it must be okay (or "hip," or "cool," or "neat," depending on where you lived). We were awash in the inflated self-esteem that only teenagers can experience. If I may wax poetic:

> We had our puberty,
> and we had our zits.
> We didn't care,
> because we had our hits.

No teenager at the time knew that top forty existed because radio almost died. No one was aware that television had captured the hearts and minds of advertisers and radio was searching for something to keep its heart beating. When my parents listened to *Arthur Godfrey Time* in the morning or NBC's *Monitor* broadcasts on weekends, they didn't hear radio's death knell. Only in retrospect do I know about it, thanks to my study of the medium. None of my high-school friends knew that Todd Storz took advantage of the need for "something" on the Omaha radio station that his father owned along with Storz Brewing. Todd Storz's epiphany while he watched waitresses pump dimes into a jukebox to hear the same records over and over is legend now. At the time it happened, who knew?

Arnie Ginsburg: In almost every market in the country, around this time, could be found a station programmed directly to the expanding teenage market. The programming mirrored the youth culture—that is, its music, lifestyle, tastes, expectations—and dreams of the American teenager. In other words, the teenagers had their own radio stations, and the disc jockey was the thread that wove together this appealing fabric. Many of the deejays of that era were mini-heroes to their listeners. When Elvis Presley burst upon the music scene in 1956, he energized the fusion of pop, country, and rhythm and blues music; teenagers were ready to become fans of all styles of music by Chuck Berry, the Platters, the Coasters, the Everly Brothers, and others, and top forty was where they got it. The rock 'n' roll radio of teenagers in the fifties had a profound influence on the adults of the early sixties. Chubby Checker's record, "The Twist," got adults all over the country dancing the twist. In 1964, rock radio (top forty) brought the Beatles' music to the country; the "British invasion" had begun. Top forty finally became adult radio, too. The appeal and talent of the Beatles attracted a wide variety of music listeners to the format.

Bruce Mims: The British invasion further cemented the relationship between radio, particularly top forty, and its young listeners. By this time, programmers like Rick Sklar and Bill Drake had fine-tuned the top-forty presentation, while Jim Schulke was invigorating FM for America's "silent majority" with his distinctive approach to the beautiful-music format—the antithesis of top forty, one might say.

Bruce Morrow: Top forty of the late fifties and early sixties was truly the first eclectic radio music format. It reached across the so-called impassable wall of age and social demographics. It offered (and still does on a few radio stations across the country) a good cross-section of acceptable music, life-style information, news and weather, and, most important, local and regional programming ingredients. Is that what a mass communication medium is supposed to be? You bet it is! Radio should talk to people, inform them, and entertain them. Top-forty radio did all of this for the masses.

Ed Shane: It certainly possessed a universality. The top-forty formats that evolved from the late fifties grew into the sixties and cemented the bonds between and among baby boomers. We may not have understood that we were to be the dominant generation through the rest of the century, but we certainly knew that there was something special about the way we were given things our parents never gave themselves. We also knew we had been given a music and a radio style that was uniquely ours. "The Leader of the Pack" allowed young girls at the awkward advent of puberty to attach themselves emotionally to the story of a fantasy renegade. They knew their mothers would disapprove as much as the parents of the girls in the song.

James Fletcher: The so-called top ten and top twenty (then top thirty, top forty, top fifty . . .) radio stations flourished around this time (1960), giving rise to the symbiotic relationship between music industries and to such abuses as payola and plugola.

Robert Mounty: This is true, but mostly top forty was a positive experience for the medium as well as for its considerable audience.

Bruce Mims: There was the concomitant rise of rebellious youth during this period, and it was reflected in the popular music that was conveyed by these emerging top-forty stations. I suppose this could be viewed as either a positive or negative thing.

Gary Owens: Well, if top forty was meant to be anything at all, it was meant to be fun! That was its quintessence. It certainly was designed to be entertaining. If the format contributed to the medium in any way, it surely was through its remarkable, and frequently bizarre, approach to promoting itself. This unique creation of radio's reinvention effort started to shake booties everywhere with its wild promotions. For example: "Wacky deejay Harold Foonman will stay atop the water tower till our station reaches sixty percent of the total listening audience here in town!" Giant money giveaways were indigenous to the format. "You'll win one hundred thousand dollars if you can name the capital of Cleveland!" Top forty was the home of quick quips and capsulized facts ("factoids" today). "Barf Mungo's real name is Spangler Arlington Brough, and he is angry today because they wouldn't let him go through the carwash on the hood!" You know, despite this, I don't think the medium was lobotomized in the transformation of the *Fred Allen Show* to *Jimmy Nurgler's Superhits.* Obviously having only a few seconds of time for spewing conversation and bon mots may not compare with the *Lux Radio Theater,* but it does offer a form of entertainment that did not exist before the emphasis turned to recorded music and less (too much) palaver.

Shel Swartz: The early seventies marked a transition in the format. Not only did the air personalities change, so did the music. I frequently read in the radio trade publications how today's program directors complain about the lack of good music product. In the sixties, top-forty surveys would be loaded with genuine hits—tip to toe. In the last couple of decades, surveys have often been topheavy, but halfway down the list, you'd be hard pressed to find really solid, hot product. There just doesn't seem as much around as there used to be. Top forty is only as good as what it has to play. That is the essence of this format.

Sign-off:

I'm fender bender, bumper jumpin', chrome cracking my way home!
                                                    —Johnny Holliday

8

Airy Personas

New Legends of the Ol' Airwaves

He's a legend in his own mind.
—Fred Allen

According to media writer Ben Fong-Torres, the term "disc jockey" surfaced in a 1941 issue of Variety *magazine, thus anticipating the approaching transition to a new age of radio celebritydom. While in the 1930s and 1940s, Fred Allen, Jack Benny, and Bob Hope symbolized radio stardom, a mere decade later, Alan Freed, Hunter Hancock, and Pete Myers would rule the airwaves. This new breed of broadcast personality little resembled its predecessor. The deejay's roots were not vaudeville or the stage. They were to be found in the radio studio— the acoustic-tiled proscenium arch of a fresh kind of entertainer. This was the first generation truly born to the medium. Through the balance of the millennium in which he was conceived and into the next, the disc jockey would befriend legions of listeners and become a staple of modern American popular culture.*

Disc jockeys drove the radio programs that captured—after television's arrival, recaptured—the medium's audience, but they also inspired criticism, if not condemnation, from critics, who saw them as one of the principle culprits behind the "dumbing down" of the medium. Observed Fred Allen, "The whole of radio, and it is a hole today, has sunk to new lows, and the disc jockey has been one of the torpedoes."

Frank Bresee: When the stations across the country started programming their own schedules, when the radio networks went by the boards, so to speak, disc jockeys became extremely popular. They became essential to the medium's revival.

Joe Cortese: They made radio what it was for young people when I was growing up. I was raised by the great deejays on New York radio. Dan Ingram and Bruce Morrow were among my influences. They helped form my worldview and kept me tuned into what was hip, cool, and necessary. They led me to the microphone and provided me with a role model for my professional future. They also instilled in me a profound love for radio, something you have to have in this business in order to be really good at it.

Peter Wolf: The deejays back in the fifties and sixties were supreme. They captivated our young minds. They gave us our bearings as well as an incredible amount of information that made it easier for us to survive adolescence.

Bruce Morrow: Well, we gave ourselves to it one hundred percent, and for our efforts we won the affection of our listeners. What greater reward? They became real fans who really cared about us. Here's a case in point, maybe not a good one, but a case in point nonetheless. Just after closing my show years back, my swivel chair broke. I fell to the floor with a heavy thud and exclaimed, "Holy shit! What the hell was that?" I realized immediately that I was still on the air and that I had blurted out a reasonably nasty no-no. I waited for the phones to light up, and they did. The listeners wanted to know if I was all right. Not one complained about my off-color language. It goes to show you that the audience really cares about their radio friends.

Peter Wolf: What makes a deejay effective is genuineness—a real, as opposed to fabricated, interest in things.

Gary Owens: Enthusiasm and sincerity are infectious. It is a unique relationship you forge with your listener—precious and never to be taken for granted.

Shel Swartz: Absolutely. The bond you form with that disembodied voice coming out of the speaker is special. The guys who come across energetically and in an upbeat, positive style attract you. The happy, carefree feeling that WRKO-AM communicated remains with me even today so many years later. It was a special station—as were its sister stations: CKLW, WHBQ, and KHJ—because of its personalities. At the height of its popularity, the station sounded so warm, so friendly, so exciting because the jocks were so prominently featured. In those days, deejays doing a remote broadcast for the top-forty stations they represented would garner huge crowds. Today's jocks attract hardly more than a few passers-by during on-site broadcasts.

Arnie Ginsburg: A lot of a deejay's popularity had to do with the fact that he spoke the young listener's language and invented some of his own, too. There was a connection.

Rick Wright: I think this is especially the case with black deejays. I don't think anybody on the air more effectively related to the black audience. There were some extraordinary black personalities in the fifties and sixties, and long before. These were real radio legends, who actually influenced white disc jockeys with their uniquely original on-air styles and prodigious talents.

Larry Miller: From my point of view, I think the classic deejay show is the result of a creative process in which the deejay expresses himself through his choice of music, the sequence of that music, and the style and content of his presentation—both live and recorded. A good radio show is driven by the deejay's ability to know what to play, when to play it, and how to present it. If the deejay understands his audience and the music and its relationship to that audience and has the creativity to present it in a dynamic and meaningful manner, then the result is usually a thoroughly entertained audience. In order to accomplish this synthesis, the deejay must first of all be an entertaining personality. He must ask himself, "What do I have to offer that an audience will find worth tuning into today? How can I get listeners to tune in again tomorrow? What makes me so special that these folks should pay any attention to me at all?" If the answers to these questions is "I dunno," then the person should consider a career in station management. If the answer is a big, egotistical "Because I am great!" then the individual has the essential or basic ingredient for succeeding as a deejay. It is called "self-confidence." The building blocks for this confidence come from having the right kind of voice for the style of radio being pursued, along with a knack for saying things in an appealing and entertaining way. Robin Williams would have been a great jock [and portrayed one in the movie *Good Morning, Vietnam*] because of his instinctive knack for snapping back with a funny line to anything that happens or is said. However, humor is not the only way an effective radio personality is expressed or conveyed. The ability to create a mood for late night or early morning is equally important. The key may be in the famous heyday dictum: "Radio is the theater of the mind." A deejay tries to create a sound image that will translate to an image in the mind of the listener. The first disc jockeys created an imaginary dance hall on *Make Believe Ballroom,* and look where that led. I've always thought of the ideal deejay as a kind of hip uncle. That is, someone who is close to you but outside the usual family strictures.

Shel Swartz: You know, stations typically impose rules on deejays that limit their ability to make the kind of full connection—that "hip" uncle—they would like with the listener. From day one, of course, announcers were not to be offensive. That was a given. Deejays have almost always had to conform to management dictates regarding the air sound.

Larry Miller: Free-form radio, wherein the deejay has the chance to fully and freely express him- or herself, is seldom to be found. In commercial radio it existed early on and then again during the late sixties and early seventies in the underground format. Bill Drake really clamped down on the freedom of top-forty deejays in the sixties. It was liner cards and shut up and spin the hits. His ultra-tight format approach left little room for personal expression. Then, as now, the creative deejay had to fight to find ways to make his personality known. He'd do this by slipping in his jokes and comments between the hits, spots, and jingles. Ironically, the most highly rated time slots were invariably those that featured personalities like Wolfman Jack, Dick Biondi, or Alan Freed. This often drove management to distraction, too. No matter how much the station executives would try to build the "less talk" format, it usually was the personality who would win the ratings. Also, when considering the evolution of the deejay, it would be a mistake to focus only on those associated with pop-music stations. There were many other music formats that engendered excellent on-air personalities. Middle-of-the-road, jazz, classical, album rock, beautiful music all had their radio stars. Regardless of format, if the deejay made the listener care about the music, he would attract a following.

Peter Orlik: Sometimes the deejay was not totally audience oriented. The payola scandals in the late 1950s showed that he could sometimes be more self-interested than listener-interested. This, of course, marked the decline of people like Alan Freed. When it was revealed that many pop-radio personalities and programmers had taken undisclosed amounts of cash and gifts from record promoters in return for giving their tunes more exposure, the knights of the airwaves lost a bit of their luster.

Joe Cortese: Listeners were less aware of this practice than were the broadcast regulators. We still loved our favorite deejays and forgave them their human failings. They remained our heroes. I think what is missing today is the level of passion that the great deejays of the fifties and sixties possessed. A lot of today's air talent could use some of the passion that Morrow and Ingram still bring to the air. WABC's program director, Rick Sklar, encouraged his air staff to adopt the maxim "Always be honest in what you say," and most of them—the ones who went on to greatness—did.

Frank Tavares: There's the belief, perhaps illusion, that some of the most popular and successful deejays of the sixties had a greater appeal or presence than those today. I think part of the reason for this has to do with the new ground they broke with music formats. And since most of those sixties audience members are today's baby boomers, their sheer numbers give a certain credence to the argument that current deejays don't measure up to the talent of those deejays with whom they grew up. The deejays today have more tools at their disposal to vary the content of their programs and to reach specific listeners. Audience research is keener and more insightful.

Studs Terkel: There may be better technology today, but a lot of these guys behind the mike are pretty devoid of any identifiable talent.

Stan Freberg: That says it pretty well. Some of these on-air guys are about as entertaining as a car wreck. There are some very talented people out there, though, but you have to tune around more today.

Bob Steele: I'll go back to what others have stated already. It comes down to being real earnest. I've been interested in radio since 1921 and, without trying, have remained in it almost since then, even though I knew I had little talent. I was just me on the air. I'm not trying to be modest, but I've always felt I was fooling the public—and my bosses. I was just a lucky guy who became interested in radio way back then, built my own crystal set, and thought of nothing but the medium ever since. Radio was who I was. Maybe that's it.

Joe Cortese: Things continue to change to the point you wonder what's going to happen to the radio "personality." Not too long ago, radio legend Scott Muni was dumped by the station (WNEW in New York) he'd served for several decades. The *Boston Globe* made a real astute observation about this. To quote: "Considering the aural visibility of Muni's former afternoon time slot, this change says something about the shift in radio management's thinking, from a knowledgeable music man to two loudmouthed 'personalities.' " The *Globe* story was referring to a couple of deejays who were fired for broadcasting false and disparaging remarks on another station. When I think back to all the great deejays who are no longer on the air and who have not been sufficiently emulated, I think that General MacArthur's comments about old soldiers is even more appropriate to this situation—"They just *fade* away."

Peter Wolf: I'd agree with what Joe says. Most of the great deejays are gone, gone, gone! No place for them today—in this current radio environment. They don't have a forum or any power anymore. Certainly not like they once had. Hey, who knows, maybe there will be a move in the future to bring that kind of talent back to the microphone. It would make radio as good as it once was. Wouldn't that be great!

Sign-off:

Yo' later, from your Wolfa-Goofa-Mamma-Toofa.

—Peter Wolf

9

At the Top of the Hour

And Now the News

> The stuff news is made of
> keeps happening each day,
> Relentlessly occurring in
> the most peculiar way.
> —Charles Osgood

Today, as was the case during the medium's initial incarnation, listeners tune radio first to be entertained and, second, to be informed. News had been an important element of radio programming since its launch in 1920 at KDKA, which featured the Harding/Cox presidential election returns.

World War II elevated radio journalism to a level of legitimacy it hardly expected. Reports by network news correspondents from the European and Pacific battlefronts made clear the value of the medium as a news and information source. By the war's end, two-thirds of the American public claimed radio as its primary news choice. With the advent of television, radio's status as principal news medium suffered by degrees but not to the extent some anticipated. It took television and the networks a number of years to put together a viable news entity.

By this time, radio had married the recording industry and had become all but synonymous with popular music. News reports were reduced to top-of-the-hour updates in all but a handful of formats. At youth-oriented stations, news was often considered anathema—a dreaded "tuneout" factor. Eventually the all-news and all-talk formats claimed a piece of the listening-audience pie, but music—replete with

*deejays—remained the chief calling-card of the radio medium, even as
AM all but abandoned music in favor of information programming.*

Today the majority of people who dial up their preferred frequencies do so for their favorite tunes. Only during times of major national news events and crisis are such well-established listening patterns altered. Yet news-and-information (otherwise known as "talk radio") programming remains an integral part of the overall appeal of the radio medium, and, in recent years, it has been the veritable savior of AM broadcasting.

One of Marshall McLuhan's least equivocal hypotheses is that radio is a sort of nervous information system that keeps the audience "wired" or tuned to unfolding events. This, says McLuhan, has enhanced the "native power of radio to involve people in one another."

McLuhan would call that a "hot" concept.

Daniel Schorr: As a purveyor of news, radio's role came with the Depression and recovery (FDR's "fireside chats"), which introduced the medium as the herald of important events. The prewar and wartime period promoted trans-Atlantic reporting, starting with Murrow's broadcasts on the Austrian *anschluss.* That inspired the idea of a daily news roundup (the *CBS World News Roundup*).

Richard C. Hottelet: I know it's been said so many times, but it can never be said often enough. Murrow set the standard for radio news. He was the best of the best. I'm pleased to be considered one of the "Murrow boys." He was an exceptional journalist and a good man.

Marlin Taylor: My first "listening" experience that I can put a date on was FDR's declaration of war following the bombing of Pearl Harbor. Radio took on a whole new dimension for me after that. It was not only a wonderful device for entertainment. It brought the events of the world into the living room.

George Herman: CBS Radio's eight A.M. *World News Roundup* and Edward R. Murrow's fifteen-minute evening newscast became the main sources of news for most Americans, according to the mail and the articles I received when I was in the Far East for the network.

Herbert Howard: I believe my father bought our first radio because of his interest in current events. Each evening at 6:45, he would listen to Lowell Thomas reporting on politics, the Depression, and the developing crisis in Europe. We listened with great interest to live coverage of the devastating floods of the Ohio River in "distant" Ohio and Kentucky.

George Herman: As to how television news affected radio news, perhaps I was too far inside to really notice. It did not affect the way I wrote the news. It did, however, affect the public and political recognition of us—the correspondents. TV gave us additional *gravitas* in gaining entry and getting answers. Politicians seemed far more willing to stop and talk to us when we represented television as well as radio. They seemed to want their faces on the screen more than they wanted their voices heard. And radio had to work harder to overcome the advantages of image over content.

Richard C. Hottelet: Television's arrival didn't cause an immediate impact on radio. Things pretty much remained as they had been until the mid-1950s. So we news people worked as before, except there were times when we were given a 16-millimeter camera and told to get some footage of the news story we were covering for radio.

Jack Brown: Radio pretty much maintained its strength in news, emphasizing its quality of immediacy and capitalizing on its position in the market as a "concurrent" activity. You didn't have to sit down in front of the radio and look at it. You could listen to the news while you were working or driving.

Bud Connell: I know radio news has long been criticized, but back in the sixties and seventies our news was faithfully programmed every hour and twice per hour in the morning- and afternoon-drive periods. The context of each newscast was always predictable and the content was entirely unpredictable. We provided "news as it happens, from wherever it happens." The listeners became accustomed to and *dependent* on our locally generated news coverage and programming. They liked knowing the *when* contrasted to today's *if.* We could be relied upon. No one can rely upon a station to be consistent today, not even a major network.

Howard K. Smith: Well, as has been suggested, when TV entered the picture, radio news began its decline. Perhaps the reallocation of budgets to the video medium hurt radio news. That would be my guess.

Ed Bliss: Radio, like print, saw the transition from wartime to peace-time reporting. Washington news and news of natural disasters, strikes, and the Soviet threat dominated news broadcasts. By 1950, I think the primary event for the radio industry was the FCC action that lifted the ban on editorials. Stations could now champion causes they favored and attack what they believed wrong. It is sad, especially today, due to timidity or lack of resources, that stations so seldom speak out. One thinks of Ed Murrow's metaphor of the sword rusting in its scabbard.

Steve Knoll: In this respect, one must lament the passing of the radio commentator. Nostalgia is not the issue here. A critical dimension of broadcast journalism has been lost—the carefully crafted essay seek-ing to place the day's events in a larger perspective. The loss is all the more acute because, while television has absorbed many of the func-tions of radio news, this has not been one of them. At a time when the airwaves are filled with the promiscuous expression of opinion by nonjournalists, the need is greater than ever for those who can apply, in Howard K. Smith's words, "a powerfully schooled and disciplined judgment" to the events of the day. At the least, we can look back to the time when such voices were being heard.

Howard K. Smith: I am reluctant to pass judgment, but I don't think our current news reporters and correspondents, in both radio and TV, express themselves as well as those who reported the great events for radio during its heyday. There are exceptions, of course. As a com-mentator, Paul Harvey is an extremely clever man, very gifted. But he, too, is from the old school, you might say. I don't always agree with him, but I'm always amused by his broadcasts. He is extremely good at what he does. A fine communicator and a bright man.

Paul Harvey: I fear that today we let almost anyone go on the air and comment or report on the news. It is not an earned distinction anymore.

Richard C. Hottelet: Well, I'd say that some radio news people are very good today, but even as good as some of them are, they really have no way of bringing whatever talents they have to their work, because their work has been fragmented and made superficial and vulgar in many ways.

Walter Cronkite: When given the chance, the opportunity is there for better quality in radio news. It is there to do the kind of work that has been done in the past. The Public Broadcasting Service provides much of what was lost. Unfortunately, commercial radio, which is most of the radio people are listening to, has virtually surrendered any idea of doing comprehensive news broadcasts or thoughtful commentary. Now it's all compressed to the degree that ten seconds is considered almost too long for any given story. You can't communicate an idea in that amount of time, much less a comprehensive sentence.

Ray Bradbury: Very true. The few times I tuned to radio news, it was all soundbites—ten seconds of this, fifteen seconds of that, just like local television news: a centrifuge that looks to be bright but is spin-drift dumb, flinging off concentration. It resembles TV's *Jeopardy,* which pretends to be intelligent but is only hemorrhoid factoids— shove it in one eyeball and out the other, or in one ear and out the other. All facts and no interpretation. I don't want to know when Napoleon was born or died, tell me about the man, who in hell was he and why. That sort of thing is never on the *Jeopardy*-type news broadcasts—a perfect example of the moronic, quick-moving visual feast I wrote about in *Fahrenheit 451* almost fifty years ago!

Richard C. Hottelet: Radio news has been cut and splintered so much in recent years, it has been trivialized and sentimentalized into snippets and soundbites. Many stories are even comic in their pre-tense at news. Back in the fifties, the work we were doing in radio news was very comparable to print in its substance and depth. We worked at our craft like newspaper correspondents for the *New York Times,* the *Washington Post,* or any other respected paper. The radio news networks had bureaus in all the important cities around the globe, and news correspondents would be assigned areas appropriate to their expertise. My story was the birth and growth of German democracy when I was over there for United Press. Winston Burdett, who covered Italy, had a jumping political situation all through the fifties, and of course he'd keep one eye on the Pope. Howard Smith was in London, and he was doing what he had picked up from Ed Murrow—the long commentaries that Murrow did every Sunday that were fifteen minutes long. They took some writing and thinking to put together. So we were producing a news report comparable to what

I believe was the best of the printed press. That is almost impossible today.

Howard K. Smith: There's no doubt that radio news has suffered in the age of television. The contributions by reporters are very short. When I was in radio, I did lengthy weekly wrap-ups of the world events. The period of the news commentator is gone, and that's too bad. I regret that loss. They turned out to be tremendously good influences for the time and the nation.

Paul Harvey: With most newscasts limited to five minutes, including commercials, it's virtually impossible to do a comprehensive job of covering a day's activities. Sadly, I must agree with many of my colleagues that much of what we hear these days in newscasts—even in commercials when we have a lot of time to think about it—is awful. Even the grammar is often atrocious.

Steve Knoll: The most apparent trend in broadcast news in recent decades has been the accusations of purported bias by supposedly "objective" newsmen. These accusations center on raised eyebrows in television or vocal inflections in radio that are said to betray a point of view. What has become unthinkable is for the newsperson to openly express opinions on the news. From where I sit, that would not be "bias," it would be commentary designed to make people think—the ultimate apostasy. In the fall of 1970, when CBS Radio initiated *Spectrum,* a series of short commentaries split among liberal, conservative, and middle-of-the-road viewpoints, CBS News president Richard Salant stated in an interview with me that any correspondent in his organization who wished to participate could do so. Of course, he added, he would first have to resign his position at CBS News. The seismic shift in the evolution of broadcast journalism from a core of learned, outspoken commentators to a myriad of anchor-generalists who suppress their opinions as part of their professional credo raises the question of whether there has been a net gain to the news consumer or, rather, a very considerable loss. How well is the public served by broadcast-news staffs who are committed (above all) to not being committed— anchormen and reporters uncomfortable not only with commentary but even with analysis? (Mind you, this is at a time when everybody else and their cousin are getting on the air to sound off.) In a

1990 address, Lawrence K. Grossman, a former president of NBC News and the Public Broadcasting Service, said "the worldly experience, background knowledge, resident expertise and significant influence" of Elmer Davis and Edward R. Murrow and their contemporaries have been replaced "by a new breed." The contrast was so unsettling to Grossman that it led him to pose "a heretical question": whether our unquestioned commitment to reporting without a personal point of view has made broadcast news bland, dull, and largely unimportant in people's lives unless there is a major crisis.

Walter Cronkite: Despite all this, radio today is still an important source of news for most people, which is unfortunate since they're getting such an abbreviated form of the product that I think it beggars understanding of the real issues that are so important to us. Therefore, radio news is indulging (in a sense) in a fraud that is really dangerous to the democracy, assuming that a democracy requires an intelligent and fully informed electorate.

Richard C. Hottelet: I'd agree with those who have said that to get the best of radio news today, one must ignore commercial radio and go to NPR. It does a very respectable job. Its news people provide a serious presentation, which is usually given adequate length. Obviously, a voice news broadcast can't go into as much detail as the newspapers. The function of radio news has always been to call listeners' attention to the fact that something had been going on or something was going on. Public radio news is very much better than its commercial counterpart. It doesn't flog the headline story the way the commercial news organizations do. NPR allows for the time necessary to give adequate detail and substance. It can go beyond the surface of the story.

Sign-off:

Paul Harvey . . . good day!

10

Chatter That Matters

Words Without Music

*Rush has captured the sense of average
Americans—that much of what we see
going on around us is just crazy.*
—Oliver North

*The talk-radio format entered the scene in the 1960s when pop and
adult music stations dominated the AM dial. In a few years following
its somewhat inauspicious debut in a handful of metropolitan centers
around the country, it had managed to carve out a comfortable niche
for itself. Yet it was the decline of the broadcast band on which it
resided that accelerated its rise to greater popularity.*

*Throughout the 1980s music migrated to FM as listeners opted for
melodies emanating from a static-free stereo service. By the latter part
of the decade, the majority of programming offered by AM was of a
non-music nature. With the repeal of the Fairness Doctrine (a law
established by the FCC in 1949 that required all broadcast stations to
air opposing viewpoints) around this time, the talk format enjoyed a
major boost. Soon there were more talk stations on the air than ever
before, and certain talkmasters were becoming national celebrities
with the power to influence the outcomes of major elections.*

In his film Talk Radio, *Oliver Stone called the "chatter that matters" format "the last neighborhood in America," thus conferring on it
an importance that many felt it deserved. Meanwhile, there were those
who viewed the format with alarm, if not disdain, for what they alleged
were its right-wing rantings. This prompted one critic to comment that*

if the format was, indeed, a neighborhood, it was one governed by conservative demagogues and slumlords.

In any case, talk radio had increased the public's awareness of the fact that the medium could be something significantly more than a record or CD player.

Michael Harrison: The repeal of the Fairness Doctrine sparked the renaissance in talk radio. Although the doctrine seemed like a good idea on paper or in theory, it actually chilled the discussion of politics and key issues on the radio. Licensees were fearful of fines and/or the loss of their all-valuable licenses if they overstepped the vague boundaries imposed by the document. It was safer to talk about gardening. The elimination of the Fairness Doctrine in 1987 opened the door to the kind of talk radio that dealt unabashedly with controversial political and social issues. That, of course, has been the foundation of the medium's success since that time.

Gordon Hastings: This gave this type of radio a new direction, which was further fueled by the feeling that the average American citizen was becoming totally detached from the country's political process. Radio, the medium closest to the local community, sensed this frustration because of response to early talk programming. The medium had long given the national programming franchise to television. The emergence of Rush Limbaugh, with national distribution and a huge audience, rocked the industry and literally revitalized AM radio. The Limbaugh show, and others to follow, became America's new form of town meeting. This programming was an opportunity for the general public to express its views and to make itself heard. Limbaugh proved that radio could once again deliver a mass national audience, and other personalities (Imus, Stern, Dr. Laura, etc.), with their own distinct conversation formats, achieved similar popularity. By 1992, after almost forty-five years, radio had again become a national medium and was creating national stars. Combined listening to national daytime radio shows now equals and in some cases surpasses network television programming.

Susan Stamberg: Talkmeisters like Limbaugh, Stern, and Imus reclaimed the importance of the medium. They reminded listeners (as well as advertisers and politicians) of the impact the medium can have.

Art Linkletter: The "death of outrage" era, whereby vulgarity and immorality seemed to be taking over our society and culture, was a primary impetus behind the launching and success of talk radio in recent years.

Dick Fatherley: In that respect, talk radio is pretty darn significant. It may, in fact, be the single most important format development in commercial radio's history. It provides a reason to listen, a reason to respond, and a reason to advertise. The talk-radio listener is in the foreground, not sublimated. He or she is in a top-of-mind listening mode. Talk radio really "democratized" the radio dial. Those stations employing this format that maintain strong production values and a steady, day-to-day menu of "hot" topics will always stay on top of the ratings race, because they'll never lose their relevance.

Alan Colmes: Talk radio gives voice to those who, until its advent in the popular culture, felt they had no voice. While talk radio has been around for years, modern-day talk radio is more controversial, more interactive, and more wide ranging than in earlier incarnations. When the Fairness Doctrine was on the books, talk stations had to do paperwork and make sure that every opinion was counterbalanced. Deregulation is what has enabled modern-day talk radio to flourish, as there is a free flow of ideas and issues and no need to report what is being said in a bureaucratic fashion.

Blanquita Cullum: Well stated. The primary value of talk radio is that we can talk back! It is all about our freedom of speech—it is our town hall—it is our chance to vent—get what bugs us off our chest. We take talk radio personally. Why? Because it *is* interactive. The host needs the audience, the audience needs the host. It starts with the provocative, opinionated hosts who talk to us—they want answers, comments—they want to connect us. In fact, they court us—arouse our passions and demand that we become players in the talk-trip. Oh, how they can tempt us with hot talk! Sometimes the hosts are so smart, we love them and we understand exactly where they are coming from. Sometimes they are obnoxious, and we hate them. We will never listen to them again—that is, until tomorrow. It is all so intimate. We care about their weight, their ties, what cigars they smoke, and if they have political savvy, they can help save the country. If they give advice on marriage, health, or the car, we become experts too. Talk radio is the barbershop, the quilting bee, the town hall meeting, and it never loses its intimacy—and we get to add our two cents.

Peter Wolf: The radio talk shows are valuable because they provide an open forum to discuss many of the political issues that exist. Because of this fact alone, they're an important programming service. Maybe the most important.

Stan Freberg: Yeah, I think talk radio is all right. It has a place in our mediated society. From a practical industry perspective, it doesn't cost a lot to produce a telephone conversation. Given that fact, I guess talk is the best possible thing that could have happened to AM, since it was fighting to retain listeners. You could say it is a form of dramatic presentation, except instead of someone like a Corwin or myself writing the lines for people, they are ad-libbing. Talk radio does get a bit weird, like that guy in Nevada. What's his name? Art Bell, I think. He's tapped into a very strange place. He broadcasts from a trailer, which is right next to that spooky Area 51 site in the Nevada desert.

Michael Harrison: The talk-radio audience, as a whole, when compared to music-radio audiences—or consumers of any of the mass media, for that matter—is a pretty desirable bunch. Research indicates that talk-radio listeners are relatively affluent, educated, and socially/politically active. Talk radio is certainly where the voters are. Some seventy percent of talk radio's listeners who are eligible to vote do so. When compared to the rest of the public, that is an astoundingly high number.

Joe Cortese: Overall the format has been good for radio. It has inspired people to become reinvolved in radio in a way that they had not been in a long time, if ever. It certainly can claim to be a highly interactive means of communication, and that in itself has to be perceived in a very positive light. Open and free expression is what a democracy is founded upon.

Michael Harrison: Talk radio, in recent years, has accomplished a number of positive things. It has provided millions of lonely people, disconnected by the cold commercial and technological atmosphere of our times, with a newer sense of community. It has inspired and stimulated millions of people to become interested in politics and matters of public policy and to be moved to action on hundreds of important issues locally, regionally, and nationally. I shudder to think how low voter-turnout would have been this past decade had it not been for talk radio. In doing this, talk radio has provided the individual and grass-roots blocks of the citizenry with a powerful voice to hold the politician's feet to the fire. In today's system in which special interests and corporate campaign contributions drive government, talk radio has proven to be the vital safety valve for the interests of the small guy.

Dick Orkin: Excuse me, but I always recall how Garrison Keillor described talk radio. He said it was "designed for two dumb shits in a bar."

Richard C. Hottelet: That may well qualify as a form of overblown praise.

Walter Cronkite: Talk radio used to be the vox populi—that is, the voice of the people—but it bears little resemblance to its earlier self. Today, its hosts and hostesses are the stars, not the programs. They seek controversy rather than discussion. Talk radio, when it is conducted with anything like a sense of responsibility, can be a very important form of communication, and there are a few such programs out there, I think. On the whole, however, it is pretty vapid.

Bruce Morrow: Clowns—send in the clowns! Sure, they may satisfy some need for distraction, but these talkers can't be real. Okay, they can be a source of information for a certain type of listener, and I suppose they are entertaining to those who can handle that kind of drivel. So—let there be clowns. This is what makes radio a great medium of diversity and variety. It provides a little something for everyone.

Karl Haas: Well, like everything else in commercial radio, it is all about money. The reason these conservative talk shows are on the air is that they can find a sponsor. That's the bottom line. Community passion or altruism has little to do with it. But, you know, there should be room for anybody on the air, provided there is a message, and that's for the listener to decide.

Richard C. Hottelet: The idea of talk radio is basically a good one, but what has been made of it is just beneath contempt from my perspective. It's just a showcase for fanatics. The so-called host and his interviewee make something abominable. Talk-show hosts like Oliver North and Gordon Liddy are farcical. I don't know to what extent people who listen to these guys are moved by what they hear. Maybe they are moved to throw up. It has really lowered the whole level of information broadcasting and radio discourse. Maybe it could best be called "infotainment," a term coined by Gordon Sauter, who led CBS News.

Erik Barnouw: Maybe I don't listen to enough talk shows, but I don't often hear the kinds of interviews one finds on NPR's *Fresh Air,* which I consider a superb interview-talk show, in which the interviewer is really trying to get to the essence of someone's job or activity and going into great detail about it without trying to utilize it for some political or sensational reason. The politically oriented talk shows, like Rush Limbaugh's and others, successfully exploit a certain political situation and bend people's interests to their interests. This is not necessarily sinister, but it certainly can be.

Blanquita Cullum: Talk radio comes under attack so frequently because so many hosts are trying to be hot-on-the-edge and entertaining. Some hosts are more successful than others. With that comes risk. It can be dangerous to do things a different way, with flair. Radio has become the alternative news source and underground for topics the mainstream press won't touch. Talk-show hosts also push people's buttons to make them react and listen. To get hooked. I often think of the movie *The Right Stuff* and how it pertains to talk radio. The beginning of the movie focuses on the test pilots—the jet jockeys like Chuck Yeager. They were the risk takers who could fly in anything at any time despite conditions. They were courageous, and yes, a little crazy. They are like talk-show hosts. Later in the film we saw the astronauts and their great training, snazzy space suits, and expensive rockets. They are like the mainstream media. Radio talk-show hosts fly by the seat of their pants every day, and no matter how slick the times become they are always a good show.

Alan Colmes: I like to say that liberals don't have the time to call and participate in talk radio. They're busy working for a living. The truth is, talk radio attracts those who are most passionate, most aggrieved, and most angry. Those people in today's society happen to be conservatives. In the sixties, it was the liberals who were antiestablishment. When they became the establishment, it was the other side that made all the noise.

Steve Allen: Speaking of which, let us quickly dispose of a specific form of "dumbth" presently common—that is, the perception that the American media, by and large, have a liberal bias. Has no one noticed that—at least the last time I checked—approximately six hundred radio stations were carrying the Rush Limbaugh show? Is nobody in an informed position doing demographic studies that reveal the incredible dominance on American radio (both AM and FM) of the most extreme presentations of the case of conservatism? I have long thought, written, and said that a sane political society needs both a responsible Right and Left. After all, the record of history as to what happens when one party—any party at all—has near-total control of the levers of government is sobering enough. But we are now presented with clear evidence that a great many on the Right—perhaps even a majority—actually prefer the rude, sarcastic, and often poorly informed, saloon-loudmouth rhetoric of a Limbaugh to the more admirable support of the case of conservatism that we expect from George Will, William F. Buckley, and Brent Bozell. These spokesmen—though one may differ with them on one public question or another—are gentlemen and communicate as such. In the present intellectual climate, however, it's a small wonder that such intellectuals are not only little admired by millions on the Right but are, in fact, often spoken of derisively by those so far gone down the road of conspiracy theory that they spend a surprising amount of their time and energy attacking such obviously conservative organizations as the FBI, the CIA, the Army, the Navy, the Marines, the U.S. Congress, and local police officials.

Martin Halperin: Radio has adopted the television-tabloid-show mentality. Talk radio is bombastic and confrontational, if not outright mean-spirited.

Bernarr Cooper: These talk hosts are mostly hot air. Rush Limbaugh hasn't done a thing for radio, even though he gets a lot of praise for his alleged contributions. I think talk radio is just a lot of hype with little spine. It really doesn't contribute anything of lasting worth. It just pretends to do so. It is filled to overflowing with self-importance.

Stan Freberg: I'm not too crazy about the way some of these talk hosts hang up on people when they don't like the direction that the conversation is headed. That is not very democratic from where I sit. There's so much rudeness on the air with these guys. I hope that a new crop of vulgar, egocentric, and obscene radio personalities is not about to be harvested, but I can't imagine that it is not about to happen given what's on the air to emulate. The radio that I knew was a kinder and gentler one.

Howard K. Smith: There's just such an overabundance of vitriol on talk radio. But I don't know that radio itself is to blame. There simply seems to be more vitriol in our society today.

Michael Harrison: All these so-called serious journalists criticize talk radio for not being journalistic. They scorn its immediacy and accessibility to the public. These self-righteous hypocrites would be more productive if they turned their scrutiny on their own profession, which, if anything, has not lived up to its stated mission to be fair, accurate, objective, and thorough. Talk radio does not even claim to be journalism in the reporting sense. The closest it comes to being "the press" is in an op-ed sense. More important, talk radio is a part of that larger social institution of the late twentieth century called "the media." That takes in journalism, the press, and a whole lot more. In America, the media are judged by the open and free marketplace. As long as the public is intelligent, educated, and well-meaning—and freedom of speech is preserved—the media will be forced to maintain credibility to survive. Of course, the burden lies on education and the public itself. If that goes to pot, then the credibility of talk radio will be small potatoes. Our whole democracy will go to hell in a handbasket. One last thing, if I may—in defense of Rush Limbaugh let me say that he is to talk radio what Elvis Presley was to rock 'n' roll—clearly its biggest star and responsible to a great extent for its success, but he is hardly the whole story. Limbaugh started out as openly recognizing himself as an entertainer. He even made fun of political talk show hosts who "took themselves too seriously." But as time went on, he started believing his own press and alleged importance to the conservative cause. Following Limbaugh closely, I have come to the conclusion that he is neither as evil as his detractors portray him, nor as good as his worshippers believe. No doubt, he has been an important player in the arena of American public opinion. If he is to survive at that level into this new millennium, he will have to back off on his functioning as an on-air Republican operative, obsessed with the conservative cause from which he seems to have difficulty separating himself at this point. If he doesn't do that, he will quickly become a relic of the past century.

Alan Colmes: As the political pendulum swings, so will the voices heard on talk radio. I don't think the conservatives will be the favored sons and daughters forever. Maybe by the time this book is published things will have changed. Eventually, the conservatives will fall into disfavor as they overplay their hand and become the very people they used to hate (just as the liberals did after the social upheaval of the sixties). Once the scandals are done and both sides get tired of bashing each others' brains in, talk radio will find other areas upon which to focus its formidable energies. Of course, there will always be another scandal.

Ed Shane: I can see the future more clearly when I think of talk radio. There are several possibilities. Questions that cannot be answered provide the best material: Is Elvis really dead? Are UFOs real? Is there life after death? How do a dead pop star, extraterrestrials, and the afterlife relate? They are all potential subject matter for individual talk shows and for twenty-four-hour talk networks. Art Bell already opens the door with his overnight quest for conversation with UFOs and insomniacs alike. Fantasy and the fantastic will take center stage on talk shows as the lines between information and entertainment continue to blur. The spoken word is the most likely vehicle for this type of content. Talk radio is where we'll hear it first. At some point in the future, what we know as talk radio will vector with the values and philosophy of Christian radio to create a new form. In addition, talk stations that turned to paid programming to siphon a few dollars from visibility-minded lawyers and financial advisors are also at the front of a trend. Expect much more of what I call "vanity radio." For a few hundred dollars, professionals buy time on their local station to conduct their own "talk shows" that are nothing more than audio infomercials. Of course, there are those who describe talk radio as just that—vanity radio.

Station liner:

Give us twenty-two minutes, and we'll give you the world.

—WINS-AM

11

The Good Air

As a Public Trustee

> *I have done the state some service,*
> *and they know't.*
>
> —Shakespeare

The government requires radio broadcasters to be good Samaritans. In fact, the notion was put into law during the first decade of commercial broadcasting. The Radio Act clearly stipulated that to possess a radio license the holder must operate in the "interest, convenience, and necessity" of the public. Failure to do so (then and now) could result in license revocation—forfeiture of the privilege to broadcast. Why does the government impose such rules on broadcasters and not other media, such as newspapers and magazines?

In order for a radio signal to reach a receiver, it must utilize the elements of a limited natural resource known as the radio-wave portion of the electromagnetic spectrum. This moiety can accommodate only so many radio signals. Since the atmosphere around us is regarded as belonging to each and every citizen, broadcasters are therefore perceived as borrowers or lessees of a public property. It is because of this view that the government considers license holders public trustees and as such charged with a special obligation to render service to the community. If you recall, many of the proponents of talk radio and top 40 who appeared in previous chapters more than argued that their special brand of radio does this.

This perception of radio as first and foremost a public service has been reinforced throughout the medium's existence, and it even sur-

vived the deregulation "wrath" (as some referred to it) of Reagan in the 1980s and the sweeping Telecommunication Act of 1996.

Indeed, the question has been raised on more than one occasion as to whether the medium is a genuine social benefactor or just another business, something akin to a shoe store. Most students of radio will recall the self-proclaimed father of radio, Lee DeForest, railing histrionically against the profit barons for what he felt they had perpetrated against his invention—"What have you done to my child?"

On the other hand, superb radio coverage of national calamities, weather disasters, traffic catastrophes, and so on, more than demonstrates the special value of the medium in our daily lives. It is during times such as these that we most appreciate radio for its human and humane qualities.

Bud Connell: We were forced to think of the public need, interest, and necessity by our fear of the Federal Communications Commission. If we were too commercial, if we were too crude, if we didn't give religious programming or agricultural news enough airtime, we could lose our valuable license to broadcast. That would be the end of a station and certainly the end of our careers. So we were careful to cover the bases, to meet the *needs* and *interests* of the public. The act of having to report programming percentages to the FCC forced a type of thinking that spilled over into general programming. The music must be moral, the personalities must be principled, the services must be reliable, the required public-service programming must not be a sham.

Richard C. Hottelet: The greatest public-service aspect of the medium is its up-to-the-minute nature. That is inherent to it and not legislated. It's a sort of sleeve-tugging medium. You hear it first on radio, then you go to other media to get the details and analysis. Radio still serves that function.

Karl Haas: The value of radio today rests in its portability and mobility. That alone makes it a significant public-service medium. This quality gives the medium primacy and even exclusivity in our culture. It is everywhere and marvelously accessible.

Richard C. Hottelet: There is no doubt that radio has a central role in our society. It has a place. It is there whenever the audience wants it.

There's an immediacy to it. Television has made us a spectator society. Radio requires more involvement, which is healthier, I believe.

Peter Wolf: Radio's most important function and contribution to society is the dissemination of information. Radio presents a never-ending flow of pertinent as well as impertinent data. Both are important.

Dick Fatherley: Peter's right. Just turn it on and there you have a cornucopia of local news, weather, and issues-oriented programming with audience participation. That's a pretty nice thing to have at our fingertips.

Stan Freberg: Above all, it's nice to have the companionship radio provides when you're in your car. That is one thing you get from the medium, and that is definitely worth something. I once wrote a piece for radio promoting the value of drivetime listening. It went like this:

> VOICE 1: The great thing about radio is that when the commercial comes on television, the fade to black is a cue for millions of viewers to get up and leave the room.
> VOICE 2: Well, can't people walk out of the room on radio?
> VOICE 1: Not at sixty miles an hour!

Dick Orkin: Radio offers programming that speaks one-to-one to the public's sense of *aloneness*. In this techno-age of information overload and distractions, radio retains the ability to reach out and speak intimately to a basic audience sense of aloneness, one that is certainly exacerbated by too many hours in front of the computer and driving solo for endless stretches of highway and time.

Herbert Howard: Other social factors have worked in radio's favor as it has become more of a personal, individual medium following the debut of television. While TV replaced radio as the family entertainment center, usually in the living-room setting, the availability of inexpensive radios led to each member of the household having his or her own set. The phenomenal growth of radios in cars and the increase in the number of portable sets opened additional listening opportunities for individuals, which raised the value of the medium as a public service. Then, too, with the proliferation of formats, radio offered the audience many choices. It is a personal medium with such an array of programming options that few people are left unserved. Stations serve niche audiences that are defined in terms of age, gender, socioeconomics, and ethnicity, as well as special interest. The underlying idea of today's radio broadcasting is that each station must develop a consistent identity in its programming at all times so as to be a reliable source of that programming for its intended audience. In overall social terms, while radio still serves the mass audience, its twelve thousand stations function as carefully tailored, personal companions. In this the medium is a highly valuable communication service in America and throughout the world.

Marlin Taylor: Radio brings happiness, joy, and companionship to a world constantly on the move, running faster and harder to achieve the good life. Keep in mind, too, that it does this for *free*. As both a programmer/manager and a syndicator/consultant, my prime concern and focus was to make our programming not only a ratings getter but a major service to listeners—one that satisfied their interests and needs. Although we were a music station, we attempted to educate and enlighten our audience concerning the events of the community and world.

Rick Ducey: Radio, that is AM and FM terrestrial broadcasting, is one of the phenomenal successes of our times. A whole industry arose that has been dedicated to providing the best-produced news, information, and entertainment available to its listeners anytime and anywhere for free over devices that can cost next to nothing. The programming provided to listeners and the advertising revenues used to drive the industry's economic engine are based on some of the most intensive and extensive research conducted on any medium. Radio is where people go to become informed and amused, to be emotional, or to just feel as though they have a friend. That is what radio is all about.

Frank Tavares: There's been a lot of increased awareness and research about how very differently radio and television communicate to their respective audiences. People pay more attention to radio. They listen more closely to what is broadcast—what is said. Perhaps the best examples of this—something still referred to by historians and journalists today—are the Nixon/Kennedy debates in 1960. Opinions about who "won" the debates varied greatly between viewers and listeners.

Those who watched had a hard time ignoring the visual impact of the photogenic, charismatic, and telegenic Kennedy. Those who listened on radio had a very different opinion. They had only the audio content—the words, the inflections, the delivery—on which to base their opinion, and Nixon outscored Kennedy. This has perpetuated the argument about which medium is the most effective and accurate for conveying the content and substance of a message.

Joe Cortese: Radio has been, and will always remain, the most personable medium. As our culture becomes more impersonal, radio will continue to serve as a place for human connection. That is its strength and its most salient feature.

Ed McMahon: It's difficult to be anywhere and not be near the reach of a radio signal. It is, as the old slogan goes, "your constant companion." Radio is in multiple rooms of our homes, in every car, and in our ear waiting for the doctor to pick up the telephone. It is played in every jogger's and bicyclist's ear and played on tape in airplanes. We tend to underestimate its service to us. It is an invisible but very present medium.

Donald Hall: My memory is full of holes about radio's past. I grew up on Bing Crosby, Bob Hope, and Jack Benny, but I never heard Orson Welles, Norman Corwin, or Archibald MacLeish. I came to these gentlemen via their printed and published scripts. I actually knew a little more about the BBC during its heyday than I did about U.S. radio during its golden age. Therefore, I'm not a particularly good source when asked to consider the historic value of the radio medium. I'm just too ignorant about it. However, I do like Garrison Keillor and one or two others on the radio today. These days, radio serves me most while I'm driving in my car. It is good to have it then.

Elihu Katz: People today use radio as a friend, a partner—a companion. In Israel, where I make my home, radio is still the more important and reliable medium for urgent news about things such as war and terrorism.

Frank Tavares: Radio has a valuable role in providing a voice to people with divergent points of view in our society. This is a good thing. Radio has become increasingly interactive in the last two decades. For better or for worse, I suppose, increasingly anyone with a message can have their voice heard. When you listen across the spectrum, when you spin the dial, you have a clearer view than ever before of the diversity that exists in our society.

Shel Swartz: Indeed, there really is something for everyone. Granted, in some areas you may have to undertake a search to find a station that fulfills your listening needs, but the variety is pretty impressive.

Ralph Guild: The medium really reaches niche groups better than any other, and it does so pretty effectively too.

Corey Flintoff: There was a time when conventional wisdom said that radio's role in the television age was to become a kind of aural wallpaper, background music for those times when people couldn't look at a screen. But I think the advent of the Walkman and the portable CD has virtually eliminated that role. Now the challenge for radio is to engage listeners' minds, their imaginations. I think in public radio, at least, we're doing that. We've got the time to go beyond soundbite news. We've got an audience base that demands more than talking-head speculation and celebrity scandals. Our challenge is to stay true to that smart, interesting, discriminating audience that won't put up with vapid radio.

Don Godfrey: The primary role of radio is still entertainment. Radio is a lifestyle medium. We seek out stations that parallel our personal tastes in music. Hopefully, this is accompanied by thoughtful and interesting personalities who entertain us between cuts of music. From a functional point of view, radio provides us with a tremendously important personal service. It provides us with direct-use information related to such things as traffic reports, weather information, the time, and so on. In times of great local and national emergencies, the medium is indispensable. You know what really makes it important to me—it is there with what I need when I want it.

John Kittross: We have all come to depend on the radio medium to get us through emergencies that range from Conelrad to last night's thunderstorm.

Frank Chorba: Radio's roots are so deeply embedded in American culture of the past century that it is hard to imagine that not being the case in this new century as well. It wakes us, informs us, tickles us, angers us, amuses us, and always connects us to our world. Each generation has its very own radio, because the medium is a reflection of who we are at every turn of the calendar and every tick of the clock. We don't grow out of radio, because it grows with us—from childhood to old age. It is there as our constant companion through time and space.

Station liner:

In the air everywhere twenty-four hours a day—just for you.
                                             —WRCH-AM/FM

12

The Bad Air

Those Tuneout Factors

We'll be right back after this time out for music.
                                              —George Carlin

Indeed, Lee DeForest is hardly the only person to complain about the quality of radio programming. One is likely to hear as many negative things said about the medium as good ones. The list of objections would probably include these entries (add your own—everyone has some):

- *Too many commercials (President Truman himself blasted radio's excessive "spot" load)*
- *Not enough news (is there ever enough news for people who read newspapers?)*
- *Too much repetition (especially on those "top-two" countdown stations)*
- *Not enough specialty programming (all-Beatles, all-Elvis, and all-Wayne Newton formats were too niche)*
- *Too many loudmouth conservatives (claim the liberals tuned to Rush)*
- *Hate those stupid deejays (not all disc jockeys are oxy-morons)*
- *Too much liberal bias (protest the conservatives phoning Rush)*
- *Not enough good music (claim all jazz, classical, and folk aficionados)*
- *Too much talk (argue Muzak lovers).*
- *So many obnoxious contests (who can't use a set of "his and her" blenders?)*

- *Lousy reception (lament FM listeners accidentally dialed to AM)*
- *Too many "beg-a-thons" (bemoan devotees of "noncommercial" radio)*

And so it goes (et cetera, ad infinitum, and ad nauseam), to quote Linda Ellerbee, who is "plagiarizing" Kurt Vonnegut—someone who (no doubt) could add extravagantly to this sad litany. In the opinion of a not-too-small segment of the American population, pulling the plug on select (would any be excluded?) radio stations might significantly reduce the level of air pollution, thus providing a genuine public service for everyone.

Howard K. Smith: I consider the horrible frequency of commercials to be the least appealing aspect of radio today. I was involved in a better time. When I was doing it, the number of commercials was limited by law. Radio is a habitual offender of overloading the air with spots.

Sam Dann: It's all economics. The idea is to crowd as many spots in an hour as possible. Once I actually counted twenty-five commercials. How often can you interrupt programming for commercials? Unfortunately, that is where the medium is now.

Paul Hedberg: At my station in Blue Earth, Minnesota, back in 1981, we had submitted our renewal application to the FCC. I received a phone call from one of the writers of a trade magazine, and he asked me if I owned KBEW. I responded that I did, and he informed me that our application was being challenged for gross over-commercialization—up to thirty-three minutes an hour of spots. I said I didn't know anything about the charge, and the writer asked if I had a Washington lawyer. Yes, I said, but when I told him who it was, he said I'd better get someone higher up in the D.C. legal system, because I was in a lot of trouble. He was right. In our renewal application during a composite week, we hit four days between spring and fall that were active for farm functions. It wasn't unusual to have five to ten paid auctions a week, and we always ran them on a program called *Auction Bill Board* at 7:45 A.M. and during the noon hour too. This was carefully explained in our renewal application. So it appeared we were glutting the airwaves with commercials, but, in truth, we really were not. The problem was what to do next to get past this assumption by the commission. So I called the head of the FCC's Broadcast Bureau, Dick Shiben, whom I'd recently met at a Minnesota Broadcasters Association meeting. When I got him on the phone, I conveyed our dilemma. I told him I didn't believe our application was fully read, and that is why it appeared we were overcommercializing. He said he'd check it out and call me back tomorrow. Needless to say, I didn't sleep a wink that night. Well, Dick called me the next morning and said that our explanation made sense and we had done the right thing in our report, so we were off the hook. In confidence, he told me the FCC was about to lift commercial load restrictions anyway. He was right.

Dick Orkin: Maybe all those commercials wouldn't be so damn irritating if they were more creative. It seems that no one invests the time, effort, or money to make commercials listenable components of regular programming. Radio management inhibits this to a very considerable degree. This is true also for all programming that surrounds commercials. Radio is utterly lacking the qualities of risk, courage, and vision in long-term problem solving. There's lots of inertia out there.

Frank Tavares: The worst thing about radio today is the pandering to certain audiences in order to hike the sacred numbers. The license that some broadcasters take to grow an audience without regard for quality or content is rather grim. This can be said as well for the deliberate seeking out of the lowest common denominator among listeners. It's easy to fuel the fires of antagonism and argument in a telephone talk show, for instance, and the resulting response from agitated listeners can be amusing, if not entertaining. However, such programming often masks itself as serious information or news programming when it is anything but that. It takes more skill as a moderator or facilitator to present listeners with the multiple sides of an issue or to introduce them to a new and fresh viewpoint. Radio, too often, goes for the easy and obvious.

Stan Freberg: The medium—commercial radio—isn't really contributing anything of much value to culture today. At least, nothing that I can think of, and I listen to radio every chance I get, especially in the car. Even the news you get is really just a sound track of what you get on television. It's all kind of pitiful. It's just reading wire copy verbatim. Not much creativity there. Commercial radio doesn't give much to the public anymore. It's terrible. The sound has gotten better, but the content has deteriorated. There's not much worth listening to, I'm afraid. You know, there is hardly anybody left in the industry who knows how to create for the medium anymore.

Shel Swartz: Radio is an entertainment medium, and because of the way it's deteriorated, music stations no longer speak to me or my wife, and our average age is forty-two. We both enjoy music, but even when there's a station that airs good music, the jocks often ruin it with their silly shtick and repeated time-and-temp spiel. It's the same old liners: "Great hits," "Hot hits," "More great, hot hits," or whatever.

Ralph Guild: I think much of this stems from the fact that there is a lot less diversity of ownership today. This does impact programming. You've heard of "dumbing down." This might be called "blanding down."

Don Godfrey: In the proverbial quest for numbers, radio programming is in a perpetual state of flux. It is ever changing to hold and attract an audience. With each change in format, as a loyal listener, I'm forced to accommodate or find a new station. As a member of the profession, I'm concerned about the trend in mergers and what may happen to programming diversity and opportunity.

Bob Henabery: Look, I know radio is not a high art anymore. It's pop entertainment and information. Despite this fact, too many people on the air take themselves far too seriously and, as such, become tedious to tune. Their self-absorption is a turnoff.

Frank Tavares: A good point. For example, the assumption is made that the majority of listeners share the views of the radio talk host. The assumption is also made that many listeners do not tune to widely divergent programming. This means that these broadcasters, callers, and listeners primarily listen to themselves, preach to the converted, and reinforce existing points of view, biases, and stereotypes. Yes, there are dozens of points of view represented among the radio stations, networks, ad-hoc networks, and pseudo-networks, but not a lot of crossover and, as a result, fewer opportunities for common experiences. Indeed, most of the advances and changes in radio have led to a fragmenting of the audience. There are more divergent radio voices than ever before but less shared listening experience.

Steve Allen: It is not only my opinion—but that of millions of American radio listeners—that the medium has fallen upon hard times in recent years. I do not use the phrase in the usual economic sense. In that regard, the industry would appear to be as hugely profitable as ever. I make my evaluation in the light of ethical and moral considerations. In the good old days, most stations adopted an all-things-to-all-people stance. They tried to satisfy many, if not all, musical tastes and provided news, sports, public service, and various other legitimate wares. In recent decades, however, the industry has been almost entirely compartmentalized. That fact, in itself, is neither good nor evil, neither a plus nor a minus. Such evaluations apply to specifics. No one criticizes the fact that some stations specialize in presenting the greatest music ever written, the classical repertoire. Others appeal to the tastes of those who prefer jazz or other forms of music. Unfortunately, on commercial stations we see a shameful overload of commercials, a frenetic rush-rush of sensory impressions, evidently based on the general perception that the average American listener now has the attention span of a gnat and an astonishing lack of interest in assorted standards and values.

Bernarr Cooper: I rather hate to admit it, but I could do without radio today. It is a medium that claims a great many things but really delivers little. It is less effective than television. TV does news better. Radio news makes a lot of assumptions that are not true. Radio will always be a secondary medium to television, if you can even make the claim that television is a primary medium.

Karl Haas: Radio's weakness today is that it gives the notion that it should just spew forth information and pop music and remain only within those parameters. It is not given a chance to flex its atrophying creative muscles. There is room for more intelligence on radio. It sells itself short.

Larry Gelbart: Radio has gone from being literature to being a magazine. Current events, current opinions, and current music—but no current creativity.

Bob Henabery: I don't get upset by the widespread consolidation that's going on or the slick copycat formats that fill the bands. However, I do get upset about how radio, along with other media, has brutalized our culture. The Carter administration nearly ruined radio with overregulation (e.g., "Changes in the Entertainment Formats of Broadcast Stations"), and then the Reagan administration nearly ruined it with deregulation (e.g., the virtual elimination of standards and practices—like ABC's minimum of fifteen percent "news, public affairs, and other" programming). It's no wonder that kids can't find Kosovo on the map, because there's no news anymore on music stations. MTV ratcheted a decade of bad taste in the early 1980s, and radio's puerile shock-talk soon followed, locking in moral apathy toward monstrosities like Simpson and Clinton.

Bud Connell: Over the last few decades, spaced repetition of records became one of the hurtful spears on which radio was hoisted. As the new wave of owners demanded more cash flow to pay for their expensive station-buying sprees, personalities, promotions, news, and other program elements were cut to allow more time for records and commercials. Music, it was reasoned, cost nothing, and more commercials meant more revenue. So cost-bearing program elements were reduced or dropped to make room for more records and a higher number of commercial breaks. Top-forty legend Todd Storz's uncanny foresight and sagacity would live for a time in the daily works of his lieutenants, but without his strong leadership the accountants, bankers, and lawyers soon took over. Creative radio with a conservative conscience would apex in the late sixties. Without regulation and without a conscience tempered by the past, the young media moguls acquired mega-chains consisting of the choice facilities in the prime markets. Most radio stations became mere money machines, programming whatever faddish noise that would attract the transient listener. They did not know how to program, and it showed. The new kids on the block embraced the facile and bizarre and aired crude Stern-like sounds for the sake of fast dollars.

Peter Wolf: Radio is over-corporatized today. It's a Wall Street portfolio item that is computerized to the nth degree. It is really misused today. Stripped down and diluted. If it were an alcoholic drink, it wouldn't give you a buzz.

Dick Orkin: I guess from what I've already said, one could easily surmise that I am not enthused by today's radio industry. Mind you, I didn't say I'm not listening, because I am. I just said I'm not enthused enough to give it high points. In fact, I could not, in good conscience, recommend it as a career choice. Today's young person, who might seek a career in the medium, is limited by the constraints of specialization and ultra-niching. He or she will find him- or herself yoked to a single format and harnessed by computerization and research tethers. Given this is the case, think about those who are just there to listen— since I wouldn't recommend a radio-programming career to anyone with a curious imagination and a wide range of interests.

Sign-off:

Aa-Wooooo, say da Wolfman!

—Wolfman Jack

Part III

The Times and Bands Are A-Changin'

13

People's Radio

A Medium for Everyone

We were radio that cared
—Dusty Street

Radio has always reflected the mood of the country, regardless of the format it offered. Just as the medium has mirrored society, it has helped fan the flames of social and cultural change. Perhaps at no time has this been made more evident than in the early 1990s when talk radio significantly influenced the vote in both local and national elections. "Limbaugh Helps Elect Republican Congress!" was a familiar refrain in newspapers and magazines, if not by Limbaugh himself on his daily program.

Radio broadcasts assisted in setting the tone for victory in World War II and—according to some—for defeat in Vietnam, with its underground-radio format, whose counterculture message was embraced by young people in conflict with the mainstream's views on the draft, civil rights, and drugs.

"Radio is the people," proclaimed programming innovator and media provocateur Tom Donahue (referring to his "alternative" broadcasts over the fledgling FM band), and, as such, it echoed their attitudes and sentiments about all aspects of life—including those that have to do with the way society operates and functions.

For many, rap music and the "rap" of talk radio have kept the medium relevant to the needs of the "people," but for many others the rap that radio offers, whether in the form of music lyrics or talkmeister discourse, is symptomatic, if not emblematic, of the puerile and inane

nature of contemporary culture. In either case, proponents of the me-
dium do not criticize radio simply because it is a reflection of human
behavior and activity. That, they protest, is tantamount to killing the
messenger for the message.

Frank Tavares: There were specific historic events that changed the way
we thought about and used the radio medium. At one level, it evolved
from broadcasts *about* events to the broadcast of the events themselves—
and broadcasts of events that had significance to wide numbers of listeners and viewers across all demographic lines. One example is the Cuban
missile crisis. The event, despite the efforts of the television networks to
make it otherwise, was not really a visual scenario. Radio's news updates
and reports gave listeners easy access to information throughout the hottest points of the crisis. It helped form their views and understanding.
Another example is the aftermath of the assassination of President Kennedy. For days, almost every radio and television signal in the country
carried nonstop information about what was unfolding. Never before had
so many people shared a single experience as it was happening. Although
the kinescope images dominate our collective memory, at the time radio,
with its mobility and portability, provided millions—those who could not
watch television—with access to the events of that horrible moment.
Much of the political turmoil throughout the remainder of the decade was
the subject and focus of the broadcast media. Activists were learning how
to manipulate events for maximum impact over the radio speaker and on
the TV screen. Of course, politicians were particularly adept at using
both. It was during the sixties and seventies that the media "blame
game" began in earnest. In other words, when in doubt, blame the
media and/or its arrogant practitioners. That was particularly the case
during the Vietnam conflict, known as the" living-room war." Another
event I will mention here is the live coverage of the 1968 Chicago
political conventions. Although the television images are what most of
us remember, news via the hourly radio-network broadcasts and special
reports provided the information that sustained us throughout the day
until we were able to settle in front of the television at night. In each of
these examples, it was the portability of radio that gave it a clear advantage over television by allowing its listeners to stay connected to national and world events during the day—while at work, while driving,
and so on. It was the connective tissue to the world around us—ubiquitous and easy to use. It was there as the fires burned.

Ed Shane: Who knew the social and political background to the rise of culture would play out on radio stations? All of my friends back in the fifties were too busy collecting rock 'n' roll records, listening to pop radio, discovering television, and playing baseball in the street to worry about bomb shelters and "I like Ike" buttons. We heard about the attacks by Senator McCarthy on the architects of Hollywood and the men and women of letters. Those attacks were conveyed in gray shadings on early television screens, not as components of our own lives or as influences on our brand of radio or our music. Now add to the rising prosperity of peace two social shifts: the quest for equality for blacks and the seeds of sexual revolution, analyzed by Kinsey and exploited by Hefner. Each quietly influenced a generation of youth ready to carve out its own identities. Some of us did this through sixties radio and, in so doing, changed its social conscience (and perhaps those of its listeners) in ways unfamiliar to it at the time.

Mary Ann Watson: The days of my radio as an instrument of unadulterated fun changed by the sixties. Reality intervened over the airwaves. Long before the decade's end, when radio finally gave up the ghost, it had already acquired its own legacy tinged with sorrowful transmissions that had helped change us. Motown hits were silenced during the nightmare of November 1963. In the summer of 1965, while in the throes of Beatlemania and completely surrendered to the "British invasion," I was separated from that radio only while I bathed. I remember a war someplace called Vietnam and that some Americans had been killed there. Before long, the older brothers of kids I knew were being drafted. By 1967, psychedelic sounds were seeping in, and San Francisco was celebrating the "summer of love." But in Detroit, whole city blocks burned and we sat on our front porch listening to the governor and the president while the National Guard patrolled our street and we tried to gauge the distance of the billows of smoke we were seeing and smelling. It was a little radio, but it carried news of colossal traumas to a bitterly disillusioned adolescent in 1968.

Charles Laquidara: The assassinations of John and Robert Kennedy and Martin Luther King Jr. profoundly shaped how we thought as we grew into adulthood clutching our transistors. There would be no way to measure or to accurately document the events that would ensue— events that would change the direction of history and the content of its music and some of its radio programming. These were the things that brought me to a unique form of radio that had something to say to its listeners and was proactive instead of just reactive.

Peter Wolf: Before the alternative-rock format came along, songs with intense social messages and meaning found little place to be aired. We, the jocks, also had a venue to express ourselves creatively and politically.

Shel Swartz: When Boston's WBCN-FM had nowhere to go but down with its classical-music format, it took on the then-revolutionary underground-rock sound, which specialized in music targeted at the counterculture. Its listeners were drawn to this kind of radio because it expressed the disillusionment of a segment of youth society. It gave it a voice that it had not had before.

Bud Connell: The ideals of the postwar youth began to slip away in the late sixties. New ideas of the stoned generation appeared in popular music lyrics that found their way onto the air. Doped-up youngsters with flowers in their hair hitched rides to San Francisco. They imagined life without boundaries, nationhood, possessions, and religion. As the seventies approached, youth's musical cry was little more than a muffled cacophony of monotonous noises, poor poetry, and guttural grunts. The mindset was "let's do just enough to get by." Let's make love indiscriminately, let's have a child out of wedlock, let's kill a cop. From high to low. From healthy to sick. From morality to morass. How did we get here from there? Some blamed the movies and television. Many blamed the radio and its music.

Allen Shaw: Politically, commercial underground or alternative radio was saying "Fuck You!" to the establishment, and that struck a chord in the hearts of its listeners. This was "their" radio station. In our most idealized fantasies, we knew that we were an on-air expression of a major political and cultural revolution. We were the baby boomers making our big break from all prior generations, especially the "silent" generation of our parents. We were flexing our muscles in huge numbers with a new look, a new sound, and a new value system. Our FM stations were a daily electronic conduit through which the music, news of the antiwar movement, and the credo of the new value system of the

Woodstock generation were being fed, like fuel, to the millions of fellow soldiers in each of our markets. We knew at ABC-FM that we were, as unlikely as it was, the largest corporate entity broadcasting the drumbeat of the flower-children tribe over powerful FM radio stations in New York, Pittsburgh, Detroit, Chicago, Houston, Los Angeles, and San Francisco. There was a certain amount of headiness in our attitude. It wasn't easy radio. On a day-to-day basis, there were problems and fears to deal with. In 1970, the Vietnam War was reaching its peak of unpopularity. The Nixon administration was beginning to put direct pressure on the media to treat it and the war more "fairly." President Nixon was already looking to the 1972 elections and had his "plumbers" at work. Vice President Agnew was attacking the media almost daily. Nixon also had Herb Klein, whose job was, among other things, to meet regularly with the network media brass to assess the job they were doing with respect to reporting on the Nixon administration. Nixon must have known that the only leverage against the networks was the FCC. It was an implied threat (never actually acted on, to my knowledge) that if a broadcasting company didn't please the president, it would have problems with the commission. It was also known that the FBI was keeping files on all the antiwar activists in the country plus anyone else whose views might be interpreted as "dangerous," as Daniel Schorr and Daniel Ellsberg found out. It was a charged atmosphere to do the kind of radio we were doing, but it also energized us.

Ed Shane: As the seventies unfolded, we knew much more about what was going on around us. We were older and more aware. We were "tuned" in and more directly involved. The same boomers who had been so connected to one another by top-forty radio became disconnected from the "establishment" by the Vietnam debacle. World events like the Arab oil embargo, the end of the Vietnam war, and President Nixon's resignation, continued to shape the nation and the content of our special type of radio.

Frank Tavares: The lessons of the sixties—innocence lost, trust shattered, the violence of divisiveness—stalked us into the new decade. Two of the defining events of the seventies were the Vietnam war and Watergate. It was the broadcast media's treatment of each of these events that made them so prominent in the national psyche. The loss of trust that many felt in their government, the questioning of authority, and the voices of the media led us in new directions. Alternate programming evolved. New voices of conscience found ways to be heard. Much of it took place on noncommercial radio—that is, college and community radio. The mission was larger than the numbers, but the belief in the power of radio actually to make a difference in our society gained a strength and determination not seen before. Commercial underground radio played a role in this, too. It confronted the establishment's politics and philosophy.

Russ Gibb: That was one of our goals. We raised the consciousness level of the kids in both practical and profound ways. We tuned them in to the Vietnam War mess and the fouling up of the environment. We really put them in touch with what was going down. It was a sort of sacred mission, if you wish to call it that.

Bobby Seale: Commercial underground stations lent their airwaves to the Black Panther Party in various positive ways. They served as an extension of the underground print media, including our own publication. These radio stations performed a service to the party, which aided it in its humane mission. They were willing to give us their microphones for a cause that everyone else in the mainstream thought was evil and tyrannical. Underground radio stations were a part of the revolution that sought to enlighten the world and inform it of the cruel and horrible injustices perpetrated against the people.

Art Linkletter: In the nineteen-sixties, radical themes were fully exploited. Violence, sex, drugs, and flower children prevailed on the radio waves. Hard rock with suggestive lyrics blasted from the speaker. By the 1970s, coarse language passed the censors. Debased social themes and gaudy and superficial lifestyles were embraced by all media. Radio belonged to the "people," but what kind of people?

Station liner:

The jukebox with a heart. . . KMPX.

14

Under Suspicion

Behind Every Set

We shall try to deal with some aspect of that next week.

— Edward R. Murrow

According to several sources, among them Senator Joseph McCarthy, the publication Red Channels, *the House Un-American Activities Committee (HUAC), and* Counterattack—The Newsletter of Facts on Communists, *the broadcasting industry was rife with "commies" (known, too, as "reds," "pinkos," and "fellow travelers") and their sympathizers.*

Everyone suspected and feared (or was made to suspect and fear) that everyone else was a card-carrying member of the party that ruled the "Evil Empire" (Soviet Union) whose declared objective was the ultimate annihilation of the capitalistic and democratic way of life, or so it was reported. It was certainly one of the sadder periods in the history of the country and its beloved "magic medium."

F.B.I. Director J. Edgar Hoover promised, "No rock will be left unturned in our sacred mission to rid the land of the godless Communist." Meanwhile, one brave New York columnist observed, "The Senator [McCarthy] from 'America's Dairyland' will pinch and squeeze that teat till it bleeds dust."

And so began the "noble" cause, as McCarthy's assistant, Roy Cohn, labeled it—or "witch hunt," as it more accurately and fairly came to be called—designed to preserve God and Country and protect all "good" and "loyal" citizens from the corruptive influence of communism. In the years to follow, there would be venom in the air.

John Randolph: There was a dark phase in broadcasting from 1950 to 1965—when the Cold War had the world in its icy grip. The word "blacklist" came into our language with terrifying results in the communications industry. Hardest hit were actors, writers, and directors. The networks and affiliates on every level crumbled under the pressure of self-appointed patriots who wrapped themselves in the American flag. The union leadership in AFRA (American Federation of Radio Actors) collaborated with the witch-hunt hysteria that swept the land. Artists who refused to sign network loyalty oaths and testify were put on the blacklist. Added to this list were the names of actors who had been on still another list, which consisted of actors who forgot lines, or who were considered troublemakers, or whose names sounded like those of citizens who testified against the state or federal investigative committees. This was the so-called gray list, which became a general blacklist and included suspected radicals—communist or socialist sympathizers or members of any organization listed as subversive by the U.S. Attorney General.

Norman Corwin: It is my considered conviction that the Un-American Activities Committee was the single most dangerous force in America at the time—more dangerous than sporadic red or fascist individuals or groups who at least are obliged to operate without congressional immunity. My authority for this extreme claim comes from widespread and chronic sources of documentation, and corroborative studies of the committee's personnel. To be called a red by that committee was usually less a ground for suspicion of subversive activity than it was a tribute to the steadfastness and effectiveness of one's fight for democratic principles. To be called a fascist by this group was too rare to be of any consequence. The committee itself was so close to being fascist that none of its actions or pronouncements could be accepted without the deepest cynicism. Let me cite only one of the atrocities of this committee in the way of charging people with being things. This happened in July 1947: The committee called upon Walter S. Steele, chairman of the National Security Committee of the American Coalition of Patriotic, Civic and Fraternal Societies (wow!), to name communists and fellow travelers. Mr. Steele obliged. His qualifications as an expert witness were that he had been one of fifteen Americans to endorse an official Nazi propaganda pamphlet containing a foreword by Hitler and that several of his cosigners were later indicted for "seditious conspiracy to overthrow the government." The "reds" he named had earned this dubious distinction by standing for things that displeased Mr. Steele. Since practically all of the name-calling, labeling, and smearing originated with the HUAC (a large section of the media being only too glad to carry the ball once it had been slipped to them by J. Parnell Thomas), it is easy to see why this committee enjoyed its abuses of power and, in its thirst for publicity damaging to liberals and progressives, was eager to attack wantonly anybody who didn't admire or agree with its aims and methods. I recall thinking back then, just as the whole terrible mess was about to deepen even further, that those witch hunters were mainly perfect bastards and thorough villains and that the accused were mainly decent Americans who had contributed much that is worthwhile to the culture, edification, or just plain entertainment of their fellow Americans.

Christopher Sterling: Clearly, few things inspired the discord that McCarthyism and the related witch hunts did. They shook Washington to its very core.

Walter Cronkite: It was an extremely harmful time in our country's history, but a profound lesson was learned, I hope—one that should last for a good long time.

LeRoy Bannerman: This menacing scourge emerged in the late nineteen-forties. What began as a congressional probe into supposed communist influence fostered by many Hollywood films soon became the concern of network radio. Wild and irresponsible accusations blacklisted many performers and producers, and, as a consequence, reputations of outstanding figures in the industry were irrevocably ruined.

Erik Barnouw: Back then Paul Robeson did a magnificent radio presentation of "Ballad for Americans." As you may know, he later became a victim of the blacklist. Erlanda Robeson wanted to hear about radio to see if she could develop a format that Paul could use in the medium. It was a plausible idea, but the rise of the blacklist wiped out that possibility.

Himan Brown: The scandal of the Hollywood Ten had some effect on radio production but nothing to match McCarthy, who went after radio and television more than he did films.

Robert Hilliard: Nineteen forty-nine was the beginning of the McCarthy era of political suppression that led to the infamous black-listing of writers, directors, and performers, not on the basis of any actual wrongdoing or political subversion, but simply on the basis of accusation by someone who didn't like that person or his or her politics. Having fought against tyranny as an infantry soldier in Europe in World War II and having seen firsthand the results of political suppression, I was concerned about the parallels I witnessed between the politics in the United States in those early days of the Cold War and those of Germany in the early days of Hitler, and I was outspoken in my opposition. The relevance of this recollection is that before I left Cleveland for New York in 1950, I was offered a job as a writer on *The Ohio Story,* for the then-decent salary of seventy-five dollars a week. I had about decided to accept it when the offer was withdrawn. A professor who had recommended me for the job confidentially told me that word had reached the producers of the program about my political concerns, and they decided that I must therefore be a "red" or a "pinko" or at least a "fellow traveler" and thus not employable by them—my Combat Infantry Badge and Purple Heart notwithstanding. Though the official blacklist had not yet begun, in retrospect I was one of the early victims of blacklisting. Instead of staying in Ohio, I went back to the city of my birth and much of my life up to that time, New York. The Cold War heated up and so did the en-fascism of the United States, with thousands of artists blacklisted in the film industry and by radio and television executives and their networks. Later feature films like *The Front* and *Fear on Trial* would reveal some of the anguish of the times for those too young or too naive to remember.

Joe Cortese: I remember seeing movies about the witch hunts where people were committing suicide because of how their lives had been devastated and thinking that something like that just doesn't happen in America, but it had.

Robert Hilliard: I listened assiduously to radio in the early fifties, where the Walter Winchells dominated the air, attacking anyone who disagreed with their brands of patriotism as "commies." Commentators and talk-show hosts who dared to question McCarthyism were immediately labeled and either censored themselves or were taken off the air. I remember one such talk host, Barry Gray, who was probably more moderate than liberal, being given the Winchell kiss of death as "Borey Pink." There was a lot of discussion of communism and communists on the air, but almost always by those whose credentials were virulently anticommunist. Only a few stations, such as Pacifica Radio in San Francisco, would invite neutral commentators and, heavens to Betsy, even an occasional communist, to discussion programs on communism.

Stan Freberg: McCarthy and his devotees, or henchmen, were characters out of some kind of surreal play. You couldn't invent them if you tried, not that you would want to.

Charles Laquidara: It's the crap that they perpetrated that contributed to the explosion in society a decade later. The fifties were a staging area for the upheaval—and enlightenment—of the sixties.

Robert Hilliard: Not only were democracy and the democratic process suppressed as the result of the witch hunts, but progress in general—even of a technological nature—was somewhat inhibited by all this fruitless expenditure of energy. In a few years the McCarthy-era blacklist would turn into the graylist, and, as more and more leaders in the field did their "mea culpas," this period of neofascism in the United States, which included the broadcasting industry, would gradually wane but never fully vanish.

Peter Wolf: I can't imagine living in a society where you were kept from working on the air because an uncle of yours or someone you once knew very casually subscribed to some labor-party magazine.

Paul Harvey: I think it's fortunate that at an ugly time in our nation's history—when a young traitor was able to walk out of the U.S. Supreme Court building with two character references in his briefcase—we had at least one roughneck at our side. That McCarthy overran his headlines and discredited himself is unfortunate. But that's a trap that tempts us all.

Howard K. Smith: Sadly, it would be a very long time before radio and television would be able to move out from under the iniquitous shadow of Joseph McCarthy.

✾ ✾ ✾

Sign-off:

It's time to blow out the candle.

—Joel Cash

15

Equality for Some

A White Man's Medium

*All animals are created equal but some animals
are more equal than others.*
—George Orwell

*Although we live in the world's greatest democracy, with arguably the
most democratic system of broadcasting, radio has not always been
what might be described as an equal-opportunity employer. In fact,
until the last quarter of the twentieth century, women and minorities
were difficult to locate on the radio dial, not to mention in off-air
positions. American radio was nearly the exclusive domain of white
males until the 1970s, yet women and minority participation in radio
has existed since the medium's beginning.*

*During the years leading up to World War II, women, African
Americans, and Hispanics found occasional work as performers, with
the first group finding steadier employment (most typically—but not
always) in clerical positions. Nineteen forty-eight was a benchmark
year in the history of "nonwhite male" broadcasting, because it witnessed the appointment of Frieda Hennock to the FCC as one of its
seven commissioners and the debut of the first full-time black and
Hispanic stations—located in Tennessee and Texas, respectively. Today, there are thousands of ethnic (Hispanic claims the largest audience) and black stations around the country, and the number of women
and minorities on the air and in staff and managerial positions in
mainstream radio has increased manifold times, although it is still
considerably below the figure for white males in the industry.*

Meanwhile, the New York Times *recently reported that "the number of minority-owned FM stations has dropped significantly in the last four years."[1] Given the continued consolidations and mergers in the radio industry, it is foreseeable that even fewer minorities will be in on station ownership in the next few years.*

However, in 1999, a ray of hope existed that this might change as the result of a possible FCC action that would see the authorization of a category of low-power FM frequencies aimed at making station licenses more available to groups that have traditionally been blocked from broadcast participation.

Paul Hedberg: It's curious to note that recent figures revealed that minority ownership of broadcast stations in America is about two percent. Twenty years ago it was at about that figure, too. Not much progress in that area.

Cecil Hale: Before the nineteen-forties, black radio existed only in the form of "strips" (blocks or segments) at a handful of stations around the country. During the early days of radio (late nineteen-twenties), black participation in radio was very minor. There were few performers (none solo) and no managers. There were no African American network solo stars. The closest that national radio of this period ever came to a black programming presence was as a caricature of American black life. Gosden and Correll's *Amos 'n' Andy,* a comedy program featuring white performers interpreting a black dialect, became the national entertainment descriptor of black life in the country. This program was wildly popular. However, it was seen by African Americans as demeaning and promoting stereotypical perceptions of black America.

True Boardman: Years later, many of us were concerned about how, or if, minorities would be depicted by the new visual medium too. The thinking was that radio as a sightless medium might be more friendly to people of color than television, and if television was the future, this did not bode well for minorities. It was my fervent hope that TV might serve humanity by helping it overcome prejudice.

Rick Wright: The first attempt at programming to black listeners occurred in the early days of the medium, when Jack Cooper and other black broadcast pioneers, like Jack Walker, bought airtime on radio stations in Washington, D.C., Chicago, and New York. These early black radio announcers provided programs that usually lasted an hour or two and featured sponsors seeking black customers for their products. The strip approach was used in urban markets on non-network affiliated stations to provide some R&B programming.

Cecil Hale: The racial mix in radio changed in the middle nineteen-thirties as the result of a creative and enterprising Chicago performer. Jack L. Cooper, a true unsung media hero, became America's first full-time black announcer. This racial change did not occur as the result of a new "enlightenment" within the communications industry. Cooper's genius was in understanding that the large black markets in the northern cities, especially Chicago, represented substantial buying power and that the path to success was in making the cultural/social link among idealism, identity, and products. Cooper became a very wealthy person because of his unique entrepreneurial vision, but his greatest success was in demonstrating that race radio worked. He was a true radio pioneer. The nineteen-forties saw the emergence of black ownership with the purchase of Atlanta's WERD by J.B. Blayton. A black accountant, Blayton purchased the station at a bargain-basement rate because many local stations had been economically forced out of business by the arrival of television. His station, the first owned by an African American, programmed music intended for black consumption, and it was highly successful in generating a substantial audience and profits.

Rick Wright: Black programming, principally rhythm and blues, was first aired on a full-time basis back in 1947 over Memphis station WDIA-AM. A second full-time R&B outlet, WOOK-AM in Washington, D.C., started operations a year later, and other stations, such as WNJR-AM in Newark, came into existence in the nineteen-fifties as radio sought out new formats to help it regain territory lost by the emergence of TV broadcasting. These stations were highly successful in creating a viable format for black audiences and also drew a large number of white listeners in the process in the early days of the nineteen-fifties. Listeners loved the great black deejays of the period, among them B.B. King, Rufus Thomas, Hal Jackson, Jack the Rapper, and the Nighthawk. A few more years down the line, the "Godfather of

Soul," James Brown, became the first African American to own a chain or group of R&B-oriented stations. His company operated WEBB in Baltimore, WJBE in Knoxville, and WRDW in Augusta, Georgia. WAFR-FM in Durham became the first black-owned non-commercial radio station in the country that was not held by a college. The station started broadcasting in 1971 and offered jazz, gospel, and R&B, as well as news and community affairs programming.

Cecil Hale: Black stations (once called "race" stations) have been the racial common ground for much of young America. During the fifties, the growth of black radio was accelerated as new AM licenses were granted. Many entrepreneurs sensed the financial possibilities of reaching this audience segment and began to acquire as many of these stations as legally allowed.

Ed Shane: New frequencies began to open up, and new radio stations began to appear. I might not have noticed except that one of the new stations was playing songs by what my parents called "colored" artists. The industry, I later learned, called it "race music." I wasn't supposed to like it. Too bad. There was Clyde McPhatter and the Drifters; the Dominoes, who also featured Clyde McPhatter as lead singer and later Jackie Wilson; Hank Ballard and the Midnighters; Little Willie John; the Harptones; the Moonglows; and a long list of others. Mixed with those dance and rhythm sounds was the work of bluesmen like Muddy Waters, John Lee Hooker, Howlin' Wolf, and Atlanta's own contribution, Piano Red. My friends and I would trade stories of the new songs we heard on the "new" station, WAOK, broadcasting from a side-street window in the Henry Grady Hotel downtown. It was a station aimed at a black audience. Who knew whether we were supposed to hear those records? Our parents reacted with disdain, of course. Not only was the music rough, sexual, and rhythmic, it was performed by black people for black people. There was no reason for self-respecting white kids to enjoy it. The good news was that the disc jockey, Zenas Sears, was white just like our parents. That smoothed some parental feathers, but hardly overcame the prejudice of the time. Sears called himself "Daddy Sears" and said things in rhyme like "Fourteen-eighty-o on the radio from the Henry Grady-o." What kid, white or black, could resist?

Rick Wright: As the black pride movement developed in the nineteen-sixties, many leaders spoke of the need for the R&B format to develop further in the area of community service. Nicholas Johnson, FCC commissioner from 1966 to 1973, was a strong advocate of the potential of black radio for educating its audience. Appearing before the 1968 convention of the National Association of Television and Radio Announcers, a meeting of black general managers, program directors, music directors, and deejays, Commissioner Johnson said "Soul music is not enough. There has got to be a greater emphasis on using R&B stations for purposes of instruction, education, and informational objectives."

Cecil Hale: The nineteen-sixties saw civil unrest as the civil rights movement, the Kennedy assassinations, the murder of Malcolm X, the Vietnam War, the King assassination, and other significant social events prompted a drastic reordering of American society and a rethinking of racial priorities. Black radio became the voice of black communities as they became volatile and reacted, in some cases, with violence. During the Watts riots of the sixties, KGFJ in Los Angeles became the harbinger of things to come as "Magnificent" Montague, a local deejay, was credited with coining the phrase "Burn, baby, burn." Across the country stations like WVON in Chicago, WCHB in Detroit, KDIA in San Francisco, WWRI and WLIB in New York, WDAS in Philadelphia, WNJR in Newark, and WJMO in Cleveland, along with many others, became the voice of reason and conciliation for their respective communities. The Kerner Commission Report was, indeed, accurate in describing the nation as "two Americas, both separate and unequal." Black radio became the best expression of serving the "other" America, which was often and historically neglected by mainstream media outlets. Contemporary events saw these stations move to the forefront of social activism. They were now seen as much more than outlets for music and entertainment. Many began to use news, talk, and personality participation in civil-rights events. They became the interpreters of events and, in many instances, arbitrators of conflicts. In many ways they became the best advocates of civic responsibility as innovative programs such as voter registration drives, health screening activities, financial seminars, and other nontraditional entertainment events became the core of programming.

Larry Miller: The involvement of minorities in FM was somewhat problematical. With the success of soul-music record sales and radio formats, there seemed to be little interest in the new progressive-rock music and FM formats in the black community. Aside from Jimi Hendrix, there were few black musicians in the late sixties doing anything resembling rock. The few black announcers I know of who did work on FM in those days seemed to be unfortunate examples of tokenism. One black female deejay (Vivian Roundtree) was repeatedly courted by ABC in New York—she would work for them for as long as she could stand it, leave, and then get talked into coming back for more money. J.J. Jackson started out in Boston at WBCN, then moved to L.A. and KLOS, where he was very successful. He also was one of the first MTV jocks and has since gone into ownership. But he was the exception to the rule and was probably denounced as a "Tom" by the black community. If there were few black deejays in FM in the late sixties and early seventies, it wasn't because they were being excluded. In fact, stations were desperate to find black announcers, to the point of occasionally practicing reverse discrimination against experienced, talented, and qualified white announcers. At one of the big conventions in the early seventies, FM progressive-rock radio was publicly denounced as "racist" by some of the black attendees, based on considerations of music programming as well as on-air staffing. Those FMers who were present made excuses as best they could but were caught in a dilemma as well as an enigma. The majority of the artists they played were white men, but not because blacks or other minorities were being deliberately excluded; blacks just didn't seem to be interested. What was overlooked in this highly political confrontation was the fact that there were, and had been for many years, radio stations that were all black in orientation—deejays and music. Every major market in the country had at least one "soul" station, but we don't recall any of them being accused of being racist. It was simply a matter of specialized programming for a selective demographic. In fact, FM rockers played a wider variety of authentic black music than many of the tightly formatted soul stations. We played blues, alternative, and progressive black music that they wouldn't touch. As a result of this criticism, the programming of FM during the seventies changed; for example, the ABC-FM group added more black crossover music, diluting the unique progressive-rock mix with pop music. In the meantime, there were other ethnic groups that also had a beef with mainstream media. Native Americans, for example. Lest we forget, too, women were not getting a very fair shake either.

Peggy Berryhill: Well, that was certainly the case until the nineteen-seventies. In the eighties and nineties we saw the growth of public radio stations on Indian reservations. All over America, Indian people are now speaking to their own communities, in their own languages over radio. Indian people are involved with the medium that has become their own. Whether it is by running their own stations, producing television programs, or telecomputing on the great information highway, Native people are doing for themselves what could not be accomplished by mainstream radio and other media.

Frank Tavares: When I was head of the Department of Specialized Audience Programs at NPR throughout the eighties, this is one of the realities I dealt with daily. My mandate was to provide programming "by, for, and about" ethnic minorities, women, persons with disabilities, children, and other groups traditionally underserved and underrepresented in public radio. I often found myself at cross-purposes with program directors in various markets trying to build a broad or large audience. I often made an argument about listener loyalty to the programs that came out of my shop, that listeners who were truly being served by these targeted programs would "find" them no matter where they might be hidden in a program schedule, the programming was that important to them. What I also had to admit, however, was that the numbers would be small, that the broadcast station would lose more listeners than it gained, and that in some instances it would be cheaper—though not practical—to mail cassette tapes to the targeted listeners. The reality was that we could reach more overall numbers of these targeted listeners by including "targeted" programming in the main network program vehicles than we could in any other way. The tradeoff was in not reaching those who might be the most devoted or specific in their radio wants and needs.

Phylis Johnson: I suppose the history of women on radio could be defined by the word "discrimination." However, those few female personalities on the air were "real" in the early days of radio. Women talked about what other women wanted to hear then—families, relationships, conversation, and sometimes celebrity gossip. The topics, of course, were reflective of the times. For the most part, women weren't trying to sound sexy because in many cases their target audience was other women—generally housewives. Mary Margaret McBride, Kate Smith, and others were pioneers and extremely popular. Indeed, contrary to belief, a large number of female listeners tuned in to these

shows instead of the soaps. Even so, by the late fifties, male programmers got it into their heads that "females prefer to listen to male
voices." Twenty years later, research, primarily concerned with the
effectiveness of female voice-overs in news packages, began to break
down some of the myths associated with the wants and needs of listeners. In the '50s, the homemaker host was replaced by the deejay. A
handful of women made the crossover. The transition meant that they
would no longer target just women. Some women did quite well.
Martha Jean Steinberg's popularity grew as she gave up household
chitchat to pump out rhythm and blues hits on WDIA, the first station
to target African Americans. But top-forty deejays like Dick Biondi
and Wolfman Jack grew in power and popularity, especially in regards
to music selection. The nature of radio was very competitive, and
audiences tuned in to hear what would happen next as the superjocks
attempted to outdo each other. Women fell to the sidelines.

Arnie Ginsburg: There were very few woman and minority deejays
on the air in the nineteen-fifties and early nineteen-sixties, except on
black-music radio outlets.

Larry Miller: When I first started out in radio in the early sixties, the
on-air people were primarily white men. Women and minorities were
used only in very specialized situations. I don't believe that this was so
much a result of deliberate sexist or racist policies, but rather more a
matter of continuing with the status quo. It's just the way things were,
and most people in the business didn't seem to think it was politically
incorrect at the time. The doors to most radio stations were open; those
who showed up looking for radio work in those days were mostly
white men.

Donna Halper: My recollection of top forty in the fifties and even
into the sixties is that it was mainly a male preserve, dominated by
men with deep voices (except for Arnie Ginsburg). I have since done
some research and found a couple of women who did get on the air in
a few cities, but by and large top forty was ninety-nine percent male.
When album-rock radio came along, I had great hopes that it would
lead to more women being welcomed—but again, there seemed to be
some stereotypical thinking that said "chicks" should sound sexy or do
late-night shifts only. I have been told my voice is pleasant, but I don't

know if you could call it sexy. Anyway, some album rockers did have a female on the air (the late Allison Steele of WNEW-FM comes to mind), but once again, most of the voices I heard were male.

Phylis Johnson: By the late nineteen-sixties, women returned to radio with a new image. WNEW-FM created "sexpot radio." All women. In some respects, the short-lived format was revolutionary. Women had found their way back on the air. But in another way, it promoted an image of the sexy-sounding female voice that would linger into the nineties. After the experiment failed eighteen months later, the only woman to remain at WNEW was Rock and Roll Hall of Famer Allison Steele. She was honored years later. Best known for her sultry voice, she read poetry in between songs throughout the night and conducted interviews with some of the biggest rock legends of the time.

Donna Halper: When I got to college (that was in the mid-sixties), the first thing I did was head for the campus radio station at Northeastern University. The program director seemed puzzled when I presented myself to train as a deejay—he said the station did not put "girls" on the air. I asked him why not, and he said that they just didn't sound good. I asked how many he had on the air to make that judgment, and he replied "None," which struck me as a bit of a catch-twenty-two. By this time, I knew I somehow had to be on the air—radio had become my first love, my career choice, yet I was being told that my gender arbitrarily disqualified me. Despite my reassurances to him that I would do a good job, the PD basically told me that there would be women on the air over his dead body, and that was that. I was not a broadcast historian back then, so I had no idea that these same comments had been made about women announcers since the beginning of the radio industry. I just knew that I wanted to be a deejay, and I was being told that, through no fault of my own, I could never do it.

Larry Miller: Women as on-air deejays were rare and were treated as kind of a gimmick, usually being relegated to late-night and a sexy announcing style. I seem to recall that in the early to mid-nineteen-sixties, several stations tried an "all-girls" format, featuring pop-jazz and sexy-sounding women, but I don't remember which city. There was a continuing preference for men's voices; it probably had to do with marketing—men's voices are perceived as carrying a certain sense of authority, which has a persuasive effect on consumers. Even during the FM revolution it took a while for radio broadcasters to catch on. At KMPX in San Francisco, starting in early 1967, women were used as off-air "chick engineers" but not allowed to do their own shows until early in 1968. However, as we in FM were dedicated to doing the opposite of mainstream AM radio, by the end of 1968, most FM stations had women and minorities on the air for the sake of creating an alternative, counterculture image. Feminism, or "women's lib," had some effect as well, although the bottom line was still influenced by entertainment factors and was not as political as some may recall. In other words, did he or she do a good show?

Arnie Ginsburg: Beginning around 1967 so-called underground or alternative FM stations featured women and minorities in their regular radio-programming lineup.

Dusty Street: Back when I was in underground radio in the late sixties, all the engineers at KMPX in San Francisco were women—young girls, actually. Then we decided that the ladies should be able to get on the air because we really kept the place operating. They gave us a show—I think it was called *The Chicks on Sunday* or something like that. It was an important first step.

Arnie Ginsburg: The mid-sixties sales departments were beginning to hire women and minorities. Management was basically white male.

Donna Halper: Even into the seventies, program directors were telling a woman job candidate that the station did not want women on the air. It was really frustrating, but I persevered, as did many other women who had broken in via college radio. When I was able to find work at the professional level, I first did overnights and was the station's music director (at WMMS-FM in Cleveland). As time passed, I noticed an interesting phenomenon—no matter how much experience a woman had, she was allowed only to be music director. I was a music director at some excellent stations, but when it came time to move up, I was asked to train the program director, but I was never asked to be one. I noticed that if a male had been music director, he was told that this experience would help make him a better PD, but if a woman tried to move up from music director, she was told she lacked the credentials because she had been "only" a music director.

Phylis Johnson: When women's groups pressured the FCC to revise their affirmative-action policies in 1971, it led to an influx of females in the industry—indeed with the largest number being hired near the end of the decade. I was one of those wide-eyed females, with no sense of what was about to happen to AM radio. Top forty was king! By the time I graduated, the disco craze had died. I moved to Lake Charles, Louisiana, to work the late-night shift at a station. I was one of only two female deejays in the market. Before and after work, I would sit in my car scanning the AM dial for female voices from distant stations. For the most part, many of the females who had started in the late sixties and early seventies were in the major markets. I would like to say these females were my role models, but to tell you the truth very few of us in the small markets knew what was going on in the big cities. We were fairly isolated. I remember one of my female colleagues giving me a tape of a female deejay from Los Angeles. I would study her style for hours—rewinding and playing the tape over and over. Indeed, the styles of women personalities differed by region throughout the country. In the South, we tended to listen to L.A. for inspiration. Deejays there had a more relaxed presentation. Women on the east coast were more hard-hitting, strong, and aggressive—a style that was rarely endorsed by most of my PDs when I first started in radio. It shouldn't be surprising, however, that some of the female deejays who moved into the major markets in the early eighties sounded like female versions of the guys who trained them.

Arnie Ginsburg: The implementation of federal EEO and affirmative-action policies at radio stations resulted in more women and minorities being represented on the work force. Eventually, the FCC required radio stations to file annual reports of the number of women and minorities employed in various work categories.

Paul Hedberg: EEO and other employee reports were added to the renewal process in the seventies. We broadcasters who operated in the upper Midwest had to scramble to make sure we had the only minority in our area on our staffs. Other than the secretary or bookkeeper, there were very few women in radio, at least in the rural areas. It was not always easy to hire qualified women in small-town radio, particularly for on-air work. In the mid-eighties, at our station in Luverne, Minnesota, we were cited for a lack of women employees in our EEO report.

Fortunately, we had two letters from women who were offered jobs at the station but had turned them down. Our intent was good, so our license was renewed.

Corey Flintoff: NPR strengthened the role of women as serious reporters by showcasing the work of Cokie Roberts, Linda Wertheimer, and Nina Totenberg beginning in the early seventies. Linda and Cokie covered everything on Capitol Hill and the White House, from Watergate to Iran-Contra, and they won just about every major award for it. Nina did the same for legal affairs and the Supreme Court. NPR brought Susan Stamberg to the air as the first woman to anchor a nightly national news program. She set the standard for intelligence and warmth that has become the trademark of NPR news magazines. She's still here as a special correspondent and a guest host. Linda's spent the last decade as one of the hosts of *All Things Considered.* I'd be hard put to list all the great women who report or who have reported for NPR over the years, but I've got to mention Sylvia Poggioli, Mara Liasson, Jackie Lyden, Renne Montagne, Liane Hansen, Elizabeth Arnold, Margot Adler, Anne Garrels, Lynn Neary, Patricia Neighmond, Brenda Wilson, Michelle Trudeau, Vertamae Grosvenor, Mary Kay Magistad, Julie McCarthy, and Ina Jaffe. NPR has also had a lot of women in key production and editorial roles, and they've done as much as anyone to shape the sensibility of the organization.

Arnie Ginsburg: By the middle of the nineteen-eighties, it was not unusual to find some radio sales departments with as much as fifty percent of their staff and management composed of women and minorities.

Phylis Johnson: In the eighties, I remember working at a Houston station that changed hands two times. For a while, we even had three staffs, and not one of the original female deejays was fired. Indeed, we had four or five women on the radio, back to back in many cases. This was a far cry from being the only female deejay on a station in Podunk, Texas. Things were changing quickly. By mid-decade, stations began experimenting with all-female morning shows, but the difference was that these women sounded real! 97Rock's Lauren Valle and Hanna Storm were a breath of fresh air, compared to the male-oriented shows with a female sidekick, who giggled on cue. Still, that's what brought in the ratings, at least for a while. Eventually, woman deejays and listeners tired of sexist remarks directed at them. Robin Quivers, the articulate sidekick of Howard Stern, softened the edge of some of his remarks when she'd put him in his place, so to speak. Meanwhile, on the east coast, Carolyn Fox was becoming known as the first female shock jock in the United States. Espousing liberal views on sex, politics, and life, she became the number-one afternoon deejay in Providence. She didn't try to be sexy. She was the anti-Rush Limbaugh. In the late nineties, several female jocks, following Fox's lead, dethroned myths of who and what females want to hear as their ratings soared in their respective markets. Today, radio personality Delilah is winning over female listeners with a mix of relationship advice and song dedications, reminiscent of Casey Kasem's long-distance dedications, but now with call-ins. Beaming to more than fifty stations across the country, she stops the music to chat with her listeners almost every evening. Ironically, it has taken radio programmers many years to acknowledge that women like to listen to women. Many of the stereotypical attitudes about women, although debunked, are ingrained in the policies and practices of the industry itself. Unfortunately, at a time when more female input is needed, the U.S. Court of Appeals for the District of Columbia ruled against the FCC's Equal Employment Opportunity policies in 1998. Six years earlier, it ruled against preference policies targeted to increase the number of women station owners. Need I say more? One other comment I forgot to make earlier is that African American women did not benefit from the affirmative-action policies of the early seventies until almost a decade after the influx of white females into the industry. By the early eighties, radio stations began actively to recruit black women.

Peggy Berryhill: As the new century and millennium begin and we find urban and rural communities grappling with broadcast technologies that promise "interaction" and "online communities," we still find radio at the forefront of human interaction. Native American stations will take their place alongside all the other media linked by the common bonds of community, and they will do for Indian people what the mainstream cannot. We will still be Native Americans or "the People," but we will not be reduced to a soundbite or a six A.M. Sunday-morning slot.

Arnie Ginsburg: When I went on the air back in 1956, it was not uncommon for deejays with Jewish, Italian, Polish, and other ethnic-sounding names to change them to something "Anglo." Therefore, my use of the Arnie Ginsburg name was not only unusual, but it really stood out in Boston where I worked. Today, an unusual or ethnic name is commonplace and even desirable.

Notes

1. Stephen Labaton, "FCC Offers Low Power FM Stations," *New York Times,* January 29, 1999, p. C1.

❊ ❊ ❊

Sign-off:

This is the Wild Child in B-Town. Yo' bro! Later!

WILD—Boston

16

Descent from Dominance

AM's Fall from Grace

> *Life is filled with static.*
> —Orson Welles

For over half a century, the AM band was the very definition of radio. It was where all listeners tuned during the medium's golden age and where the overwhelming majority tuned after its subordination by television as the prime source of home entertainment.

From 1950 to 1980 the number of AM stations burgeoned to the point of near saturation. Anyone with a desire to own a radio facility sought an AM signal because it was where the money was to be made. In fact, the demand for AM frequencies reached such a fever pitch in the early '60s that the FCC was prompted to impose a freeze on license issuance in order to sort things out. It was the "hot" radio medium during the time when FM searched for an identity that would give it the kind of currency it needed to attract a more meaningful (salable) block of listeners.

As late as the 1970s, an indication of the demand for AM frequencies was the country's move at the World Administrative Radio Conference (WARC), held in Europe, to have the band extended so that minorities could get in on station ownership—something they had been denied due to long-prevailing social and economic strictures.

However, by the time this plan was to be implemented, FM had reduced the amount of AM listenership to a fraction of its previous size. The eldest electronic mass medium had hit on hard times, and in the 1980s and early1990s hundreds of AM outlets (mostly those with low power and limited operating schedules) went silent.

Despite this, today many AM stations continue to top the ratings in their respective markets and command vast sums of money when they are sold, and with the potential of the playing field being leveled somewhat with the conversion of radio from analog to digital, AM is still alive and transmitting.

Stanley Hubbard: The sixties really marked the proliferation of transistor radios, high-power electric transmission lines, and neon advertising signage. This is all very important and little understood in relation to the AM radio medium. The high-power electric transmission lines and neon signs created huge interference problems for the reception of AM signals, especially on the high end of the dial. Then when transistor radios came along, particularly the cheap ones from Japan, the linear dial disappeared from less expensive and easily accessible radios. This was disastrous for stations such as KSTP-AM, which was located at 1500 on the dial, and very helpful to WCCO-AM, located at 830 on the dial. At the same time, to complicate matters, the FCC was granting many licenses for new stations up in the 1200 kilocycles and higher end of the dial. The result was that on radios with nonlinear dials these stations (because they were squeezed closer together and there were more of them) became very difficult to tune in. It was a very serious problem. As I already mentioned, as high-tension lines were spread across the country—with hundreds of thousands of volts of electricity shooting down them—further station interference plagued the high end of the AM dial.

Lynne Gross: What really kept AM at a disadvantage was the FCC's refusal to rule on stereo for the band early on. This may have kept it from catching on.

Christopher Sterling: This no doubt had an effect. By the time the commission got around to assigning a standard, it was a case of too little, too late. When AM stereo got its formal go-ahead in the mid-nineteen-nineties, it hardly mattered.

Peter Orlik: A stigma became attached to the AM medium. When three quarters of the listening audience was tuned to FM in the late nineteen-eighties, AM had come to be labeled "antique modulation."

W.A. Kelly Huff: I've made this subject the focus of my research over the past few years. So, if I may, let me give you my take on it, and excuse me if I get a bit long-winded. Here goes. Aside from the introduction of television, perhaps the most important change for radio came in the late nineteen-seventies and early nineteen-eighties, when FM ended AM's reign. AM had always commanded the vast majority of listeners, but in 1979 FM reversed that trend. Despite the fact that AM stations outnumbered FM stations in the nineteen-eighties, the latter now led in audience size. Technology has always played a central role in the development of radio. The quest for aural perfection has resulted in numerous advances. Since FM's ascent in the late seventies, many AM broadcasters have tried to avoid the issue of improving sound quality and technology by altering programming, such as switching from music-oriented formats to voice-only programming like news and talk. But eventually they took a two-pronged approach to reversing their shrinking fortunes. This not only included adjusting their programming, but acknowledged the need to enhance AM's sound quality and technical service through stereo transmission. Initially, stereo was considered the great savior of AM, but because the FCC botched the standard-setting process, the technology never helped. Various industry factions lobbied for one or another of five competing systems proposed by Belar, Kahn, Motorola, Magnavox, and Harris. The FCC grappled with the question of which would best serve the public's interest. In 1980, the commission tentatively chose Magnavox as the standard, and this fact was leaked to the trades. Tremendous negative feedback ensued, forcing the FCC to reconsider its decision and to resume the selection process under the increased scrutiny of the trades. Unable to make a decision, in March 1982 it announced that the decision would be left to the marketplace, concluding that this would take care of any existing deficiencies that existed. This action was perceived, at least at the outset, as a bold and fresh step by the commission. It was the first time the industry was forced to establish its own transmission standard. Many in the industry, however, believed the commission's action left the medium in a hopeless quandary, because each of the five systems was incompatible with the others—meaning that only a receiver employing the same technology could decode that system. Despite this, the FCC appeared confident that the best system would prevail and that no preferential treatment should be given the matter. Those in the business of AM broadcasting and receiver manufacturing did not share the commission's optimism. Realizing that the marketplace might eventually filter out one or more of the systems, most of the stations and manufacturers were reluctant to align with any one. As a result, only a few receivers were built with the stereo feature and only a few AM stations broadcast in stereo. Within two years after the marketplace decision, Motorola and Kahn were the only systems remaining. Surprisingly, receivers capable of decoding all five systems emerged but were unsuccessful. Over the years, a number of broadcast-industry players petitioned the FCC to reconsider the issue. Legally obligated to answer these petitions, the commission purposely delayed public comment until 1988 when it could deny them all in one tidy proceeding. The commission proclaimed that there was no need to intervene because, in its opinion, the marketplace approach was working out. Citing Motorola's lead over Kahn as evidence, it declared the Motorola system the de facto standard. Nonetheless, the Kahn company refused to concede, leaving the AM stereo standard question still unanswered. On October 25, 1993, the commission adopted a Report and Order that made Motorola's C-QUAM system the official standard for AM stereophonic broadcasting in the United States. Ultimately the AM industry itself realized that adding stereo to poor existing technology would not matter a whole lot. The basic AM service itself needed improvement. The FCC stepped in to set National Radio Systems Committee (NRSC) standards to aid in that effort. Today AM can claim around twenty percent of the listening audience pie without widespread use or application of stereo, and the medium has kind of stabilized at that level. For a while it looked as though the band would not even survive.

Gordon Hastings: When FM grabbed up the music listener, AM was left to find a new programming direction it could accommodate with what it had to offer as a somewhat inferior system of broadcasting.

Michael Harrison: As has already been suggested, this period is when talk radio came into play. It is the format that clearly saved AM from becoming obsolete way before its time. It revived the concept of the radio "personality" and the radio "star." And it created an amazingly effective, cost-efficient vehicle for direct response advertising.

Bruce Mims: That's a fair assessment. Certainly, as the migration of music-based formats continued, the AM service found it necessary to reorient itself. Fortunately, it had talk-based programming on which to focus. The popularity of Rush Limbaugh's weekday program—along with the programs of a host of other talkers—is credited with revitalizing the declining medium.

Sam Sauls: Call it a case of good timing, but the increased popularity of talk-show programs and personalities came to AM's rescue. If ever there was a time when talk wasn't cheap, it was when AM was about to go down for the count. Many critics complain of the content of talk radio—"shocking," cried some—but people were listening again.

Stanley Hubbard: I have to return again to the issue of cheap radio receivers and their impact on AM reception. Around 1980 we started to see a turnaround for AM stations like KSTP because with the advancement of technology, manufacturers were once again starting to improve the quality of radio receivers. Around this time, too, automobile manufacturers began the installation of better AM radios—radios that were able to distinguish one frequency from another, which made tuning much easier. This, along with some other positive things, has resulted in a resurgence of AM's popularity and an overall stronger radio industry.

Peter Orlik: It appears some owners are keeping their AM operations alive only to have something to exchange for a digital frequency assignment when DAB (digital audio broadcasting) becomes a reality.

W.A. Kelly Huff: At this stage, the bad news about DAB is that it appears to be yet another example of the FCC's indecisiveness. The good news about DAB is that it offers great promise for an ailing radio medium—that is, one that is losing some of its technical relevance in light of global digitalization. When, and if, the conversion of radio to the digital domain takes place, it may keep AM from becoming extinct once and for all. Great fidelity will be a nice plus, but for me it will never replace the countless wonderful hours I spent at night listening to AM radio from faraway places. The static only added to its character.

Sign-off:

Wishing you a big fat, ever-lovin', blue-eyed (SFX: Reverb) BYE NOW!!

—Peter Martin

17

Ascent of Fidelity

FM's Rise to Power

> *The biggest problem I can see is the elimination of static.*
>
> —Edwin Armstrong

There is rather a macabre (as well as uncorroborated) tale surrounding the suicide of FM radio's inventor. Allegedly, upon hearing of the death of Edwin Armstrong, his opponent during years of heated litigation, RCA's David Sarnoff, snidely remarked, "I guess he couldn't take the static." Ironically, it was the "static" (to which Sarnoff supposedly alluded) that inspired Armstrong to reach for the sky rather than leap to the ground.

Until the 1950s, except for a modest cadre of audiophiles, the general public had little awareness or appreciation of or interest in FM broadcasting. Television's arrival deepened this indifference even further, at least for a while. The prevailing attitude was: "Who cares about improved radio reception when there is television to watch? Besides AM is just fine when you want to tune the 'sightless' medium."

Later in the 1950s, the recording industry marketed "hi-fi" albums, and FM broadcasters aired them over their sharper and clearer frequencies. This attracted more fans to the static-free listening option. Most FM programming was less mainstream in nature, and due to its "fine-arts" scheduling (classical, opera, and jazz music and discussion programs focusing on cultural themes), it acquired the reputation and image of being radio designed for "eggheads"—intellectuals smoking pipes and reading Sartre.

In the early 1960s, stereophonic sound was embraced by the FM band, and it proved to be the single most significant factor in the medium's ascent to high ratings and large audiences. There was other help along the way. The FCC imposed a rule that required AM/FM combo operators to originate programming on their FMs rather than duplicate their AM broadcasts. This gave rise to the "less-talk, more-music" programming formula that eventually enticed many listeners (typically over forty years old) to abandon the cluttered—spot- and chatter-ridden—AM sound.

However, the defining event that propelled FM to dominance was its scheduling of youth-oriented pop music (rock) in the 1970s. By the decade's end, the medium, which had lived in the shadow of its AM radio sibling, for so many decades, became the preferred band for the majority of listeners.

Marvin Bensman: During the early years of FM, stations were programmed independently, although many were owned by licensees of AM stations and operated in the same markets, and even the same studios, as their AM big brothers. Within a year or two, however, virtually all of the FM stations that were connected with AMs adopted the policy of simply duplicating—simultaneously—the programs by their AMs. Their owners had not been successful in selling enough time on the FM stations to pay operating costs, and duplication of service cut costs. Over two hundred twelve FMs went off the air in 1949.

Irving Fang: General Electric, Zenith, and other companies were starting to build FM bands into their radio sets along with the AM and shortwave bands. Armstrong's excellent but frustrated technology had the potential to render all existing radios obsolete, although not everyone would have subscribed to that notion, especially in the midst of ongoing court battles with RCA. FM stations came and, toward the end of the period, went.

W.A. Kelly Huff: As I know has been said earlier, for its first several years, if not decades, FM radio languished in the shadow of AM. Several factors helped change this situation, but they did not occur until the late fifties and early sixties. One of the things that helped FM was the clogging of the AM spectrum space. As room became scarce, the FCC became stingier with allocations and all but stopped licensing

AMs. This inspired growth on the FM side, because frequencies could be found there.

Marlin Taylor: When I finished my stint in the army, producing recruitment radio shows, I became the program director for WHFS-FM in Maryland. It went on the air as the first stereo station in the nation's capital. It was 1961. Since the equipment manufacturers were just beginning to make gear for stereo broadcasting, much of our equipment was home-built or specially modified. Our stereo generator was a test device created by H.H. Scott (a leading hi-fi-component manufacturer of the day) and designed by them to test their new stereo FM receivers. FM was still the infant radio medium at this time. Many of the stations that were on the air simply duplicated their AM relatives. Most independently operated stations broadcast classical or Muzak-like musical programming. We at WHFS, as a pioneer FM stereo outlet, sought to satisfy many musical tastes by airing not only classical, but segments of contemporary jazz, Dixieland jazz, Broadway show tunes, and Enoch Light-style recordings as well.

Bruce Mims: Certainly television's introduction just prolonged FM's notice, although the FCC's allowing the medium to use its subcarrier (SCA) to provide other services helped it keep its nose above water early on.

Christopher Sterling: Because of the logjam on the AM band, FM was the only way to get new stations into major markets.

Paul Hedberg: A good point, indeed, and another thing that helped FM spread its wings is the fact that many operated in local communities as a way to provide their AM counterparts with the illusion of full-time service, since many had daytime-only licenses. I remember joining the National Association of FM Broadcasters, a group outside of the National Association of Broadcasters. The FM broadcasters group felt that FM owners were not being served by NAB. We were all small-market AM operators trying to promote FM. Of course, if you had a full-time AM radio station that covered the market, you didn't have much interest in adding an FM, so we FM broadcasters were a relatively small group. It stayed that way until the seventies when big-city broadcasters were forced to take a closer look at the medium because of its increasing popularity as a source for stereo music. Most of the big AM operators were dragged into FM kicking and screaming. Since my FM stations were in small farm markets, I began to search for other ways to generate revenue. Enter the nice by-product of FM stereo development—the subcarrier of FM stations. I couldn't employ Muzak because another station had it already, so I came up with the idea of running the Chicago Board of Trade and Merchandise results, something all local grain dealers relied on daily to set their prices. I was on to something, and it quickly proved tremendously successful. What I did was send three schoolteachers out during the first summer to call on the grain dealers and tell them of the service that would give them the grain markets every five minutes on a speaker in their office. The teachers sold three hundred accounts at thirty dollars per month. With this, at our station in Blue Earth, Minnesota, I formed a company, Market Quoters Inc., which featured an announcer reading the markets from Chicago. Eventually we had nearly one thousand customers. In 1967 the FCC approved data transmission on SCAs. We joined another operator and programmed a computer so we could put the market on a screen, and, with this, we increased our price to one hundred sixty dollars a month. Within three months we discontinued the voice service for the data. Several other companies copied my idea throughout the Midwest and operated in different territories. However, the first FM-SCA transmissions of farm markets originated in Blue Earth, Minnesota, in October 1972. I operated the company until 1996 when we sold it to Data Transmission Network in Omaha.

Frank Tavares: The commercial stations where I worked in the sixties were AM. In each case, however, the station held an FM license as well. For the first part of the decade, the FM broadcasts simply mirrored that of their older AM sibling. The stations "simulcast' their programming, and it was only during the station breaks that listeners to either signal were given a clue that this was happening. The announced call letters were followed with "AM and FM." It was cheap and easy to do. Fewer listeners had FM receivers in comparison to AM, and those sets were not portable. It made little sense to put money and talent into the FM, despite its clearer signal. Commercials that an advertiser bought on the AM also ran on the FM at no extra charge— as a bonus of sorts. But broadcast regulations changed, and in the second half of the decade, there was a limit on how many hours per day an AM station could duplicate its programming on FM. From my on-air-talent point of view, this is when we began to think differently about the FM signal. How could we fill those extra hours without detracting from the AM money-maker? To make matters worse, the AM on-air talent saw working on the FM side as a demotion and demoralizing, even with the incentive of overtime pay. Initially, the FM slots were given to those lowest on the totem pole—a good way to train greenhorns with little consequence to listeners if they messed up. This should give you a sense of the status of FM broadcasting in the nineteen-sixties and earlier.

Marvin Bensman: FM broadcast in monaural until the FCC approved of its broadcasting in stereo after a brief period of experimentation in 1960. Stereo records and phonographs for the home had been introduced a couple of years before. In 1957 FM accounted for only two percent of radio sales but increased to 10 percent in 1960.

James Fletcher: Something that may or may not have been mentioned as contributing to the emergence of FM is the FCC's mandate that radio receivers be all-frequency, not just AM, which is what most were around this time.

Peter Orlik: FM prospects were finally looking up when the FCC authorized the Zenith-General Electric system for transmission of stereophonic sound. This created a product that grabbed the attention of the public.

Christopher Sterling: At the same time, the development of the high-end hi-fi movement as a subset of consumer electronics really was helped or paced by major-market classical FM stations.

Robert Mounty: The vastly improved sound through FM's cleaner reception and capacity for stereo broadcasting was a very positive plus, in general, for the radio industry at a time when it needed a boost.

Newton Minow: Stereo FM really exploded in the sixties and seventies. It helped put FM on the map.

Bruce Mims: Dual policy decisions by the FCC infused new life into FM. By authorizing multiplex (stereophonic) broadcasting and by curtailing the amount of AM programming duplication over FMs, the commission's actions resulted in a significantly enhanced broadcast service.

Gordon Hastings: The second renaissance in radio came in the 1970s, and it was once again driven by music. FM signals, long overlooked by mainstream broadcasters, became the new delivery system for music programming. Stereo and superior sound quality drove nearly all music to the FM band back then, and it has remained there ever since. Ironically, initially at least, the big push for FM was not delivered by pop or contemporary music as it had been on AM, but by a format that was called beautiful music. Vast audiences were amassed almost overnight on stations programmed by Jim Schulke and Marlin Taylor. Another early entrepreneur who saw this opportunity was Woody Sudbrink, who, in less than a year, built the largest group of number-one-rated FM-only stations in major markets. Once it was proven that the FM band would attract big audiences, all-music programming followed. By the late 1970s, the numbers were astronomical for FM. Curiously, at that time, 90 percent of all FM listening was done on a monophonic radio. AM radio was left to find a new direction.

Lynn Christian: When you have survived for four decades in radio, starting as a twenty-year old deejay on a Texas AM station while a student at the University of Houston, you look back at the people who made the voyage with you and try to place a fix on the exact period in your career that you found most exciting. In my case, it was the sixties. No, not the anti-Vietnam, Woodstock, sexual revolutionary, AM-rock 'n' roll-radio sixties you usually hear about. I'm referring to the low-key, sophisticated, innovative, and cutting-edge stereo-FM radio we youthful entrepreneurs produced for dissatisfied listeners who were ready to abandon their AM stations with their loud promotions, heavy spot loads, and music repetition. I happily admit to being a part of that enthusiastic band of early FM broadcasters in both Houston and New York City. In the latter locale, at WPIX-FM (now WQCD), we called what we aired "The Sound of the Good Life from the PIX Penthouse." At Houston's KODA-FM, we called what we did "The Velvet Touch." During those seven great years (1962 through 1968) of early FM stereo, we made wonderful connections with our adult (aged twenty-five plus) listeners. The smooth non-rock mix of instrumentals and vocal music, highlighting great new Burt Bachrach and Cy Coleman songs from Broadway, mixed with past hits, a few rock "covers," and a splash of Latin and jazz selections not being aired by AM, was what constituted our format. Our mission was to bring down the high-pitched tempo of radio with a more relaxing bed of music; soft, friendly voices; and fewer commercials. It was all very "quality" conscious and "quality" controlled. There has never been a more comfortable format than this one, which was created, produced, and manicured daily by my longtime friend, Charlie Whitaker, and syndicated to FM stations in the late sixties and early seventies. We weren't alone, however. Jim Schulke, Marlin Taylor, Darrel Peters, and other syndicators came along soon with their own take on the stereo beautiful-music format. In New York in 1967, WPIX-FM had the number-one Arbitron-rated audience of eighteen- to-forty-nine-year-old adults at a time when just sixty-five percent of homes and fewer than twenty-five percent of cars had an FM receiver. As broadcasters, we were privileged to be a part of fun that was not based on sophomoric shopping-center promotions or mean-spirited pranks aimed at other competing AM radio stations. In the early days in Houston and New York, all of the independently programmed FM stations worked together promoting FM stereo radios for homes and cars. Thanks to my Houston mentor, friend, and owner of KODA, Paul Taft, we produced a monthly program guide, which for three years kept us in touch with our listeners and gave me an opportunity to spend time with many of the world's great musicians, like Leopold Stokowski (then music director of the Houston Symphony Orchestra), who willingly posed for a cover and then spent hours with Ron Schmidt, our program director, and myself sitting at a neighborhood drugstore counter talking about our young children and the future of contemporary music in America. Later, in New York, I looked forward to having lunch on Fridays in the *Daily News* dining room on Forty-second street with John Lissner of McGraw-Hill, who served as host of his Saturday night jazz show, which often featured great legends of jazz and big band. Working in our kind of FM back then was wonderful for us and wonderful for our listeners. Great conductors, world famous jazz figures, key news figures, and Broadway artists were what our new stereo FM was about. Our audience respected our stations, our personalities, and the intelligence of our presentations. I consider this phase in the history of American broadcasting as radio's renaissance. If you didn't have the good fortune to participate in it as a broadcaster or listener, you missed something special. Sorry! Most of us were not in it for financial reasons; those rewards took a long time to arrive. We just loved the new sound of stereo FM after years of listening and working with one-dimensional AM programming. It was an era, I believe, that had a major role in shaping the values at FM stations today.

Marlin Taylor: Just to give you a statistical perspective on all this: According to the FCC, there were four thousand two hundred and forty-nine AM stations in August 1968. Meanwhile, there was less than half that number of FM outlets, two thousand and thirty-eight— not including three hundred eighty-two educational FM stations.

Ed Shane: The rise of FM paralleled the expansion of choice that the baby-boomer population grew to expect. Rock split to accommodate different ears. Adult contemporary was born of the need for something softer than rock but not so sleepy as the lush background instrumentals of beautiful music. Top forty gave way to a narrower list of hot hits.

Larry Miller: The emergence of FM album-rock formats allowed deejays to claim greater control over their airtime. Those of us who worked in FM in the late sixties and early seventies came from a variety of radio backgrounds. Many of us were top-forty dropouts who reveled in the opportunity to throw away the playlists and create our own show everyday. Other deejays came from the street and brought with them good instincts and a good record collection as well as a breath of fresh air by providing a natural (humanized) deejay style in stark contrast to the "stilts" in other formats. Others, like myself, came from what might be called a fine-arts background. We all had one thing in common: We had grown up listening to true radio personalities and were motivated by a strong desire to do the same as they had done—only with hipper music. I had worked with a wide variety of music but had my best opportunities while playing folk and classical at WDTM in Detroit in the mid-nineteen-sixties. I developed a free-form folk show that aired every afternoon, and it was that experience that I took with me to San Francisco and that guided my efforts, in February 1967, on KMPX which became the nation's premiere underground/progressive station. Keep in mind, all this exploration and experimentation on the air was made possible because of FM's existence at the time. You listen to FM today, and you quickly realize things have changed. FM is now pretty much what AM used to be when it aired music.

James Fletcher: The rise in the number of well-managed FM radio station groups or companies got FM in the profit margins. One example was the successful Bonneville FM stations. There were numerous others. Around 1980, the medium had certainly come into its own with impressive advertising rates and the increased availability of high-quality home and auto receivers.

Stanley Hubbard: We finally began to see the meaningful and profitable development of our FM radio services. It became a real success story.

Sign-off:

May each and everyone one of you find a little pot at the end of your rainbow.

—Larry Miller

18

Shock Waves

Polluting the Air

So take off your panties and fart into the mike.
—Howard Stern

When actress Mae West appeared in a 1937 network radio skit about the seduction of Adam by Eve, a social uproar ensued, and she was banished from the medium for nearly four decades. Her transgression involved sexual innuendo that by today's standards would hardly earn a PG rating. Now, far worse is routinely heard on radio stations across America each day.

The Federal Communications Commission has always been particularly sensitive about profane material over the airwaves, yet off-color broadcasts have been a fact of life almost since the medium's inception. As one critic recently put it, "This is just another aspect of society that radio mirrors—one which many would like covered with a scarlet blanket."

The controversy began to percolate with greater ferocity during radio's first full postwar decade when parents condemned radio stations for airing rock 'n' roll songs, which they claimed were leading their sons and daughters down the road to perdition. In the 1960s, caustic talk-show host Joe Pyne came under fire for programs featuring prostitutes and homosexuals engaged in graphic discussions of their lifestyles.

The 1970s saw the issue heat up even further when "topless radio" swept the nation. The format involved callers describing in poignant detail their sexual fantasies, experiences, and problems to program

hosts. The FCC quickly intervened, and stations, fearing costly repri-
sals by the commission, pulled the plug on the genre.

Perhaps no so-called X-rated radio broadcast is as notorious as
comedian George Carlin's "Seven Dirty Words" routine ("I was
thinking one night about the words you couldn't say on the public
airwaves . . ."), which was broadcast over New York station WBAI in
the 1970s. It resulted in litigation (FCC v. Pacifica) *that reached as far*
as the nation's highest court.

Still all of this pales by comparison to what surfaced in the
1980s: "raunch radio," which inspired the FCC to levy steep fines
against those—in particular Howard Stern—who broadcast what it
somewhat vaguely defined (prompting a controversy of its own among
First Amendment advocates) as "obscene and/or indecent" material.

Despite actions by the commission, this kind of programming did
not go away. In fact, today the reputed "shock jocks of raunchy radio"
have legions of loyal fans and high ratings in cities across the country,
and their attitude toward those who take umbrage at what they do over
the air is perhaps best summed up by the self-proclaimed "king of all
media," Howard Stern, in a conversation with a disgruntled caller:
"Hey, dial another F—ing station . . . fool! Don't mess with my free-
dom of speech . . . A—hole!"

Peter Orlik: The Supreme Court's ruling in the 1978 Pacifica case
established that the FCC had the power to regulate indecency over the
airwaves. At issue was a broadcast by Pacifica Foundation station
WBAI in New York of an album monologue by George Carlin. In an
afternoon drive with his fifteen-year-old son, a parent heard the broadcast over the car radio and complained to the FCC. The Supreme
Court's affirmation of the commission's subsequent sanctioning of the
station reiterated that broadcast content could be more restricted than
that found in print. This did not make some broadcasters very happy.

Bernarr Cooper: Well, so what? That kind of prurient programming
doesn't add anything at all to our society or culture. I really don't see
any place for it, so the FCC is working in the public's interest by
keeping such vile stuff to a minimum.

Sam Dann: The climate exists for this kind of radio because moral,
ethical, and even intellectual standards have all but disappeared. Look

around outside of radio, too. What kinds of books are best-sellers? Aren't the most popular movies the ones that deal with over-the-top violence, explicit sex, and the most simplistic and embarrassing sentimentality? Not to mention the most sophomoric form of humor. It is all rather debasing, and you can easily dial it up anytime you want.

Paul Harvey: Our beautiful language has meant so much to us. It has profited and prospered our family. For anybody to dirty it up, for anyone to drag his bedroom into my environment, I find inexcusable. But my observation of history over the years suggests that such on-air excess, or any kind of excess for that matter, ultimately is its own undoing. Things always go too far, it seems. And I'm wondering if the next focus by our powerful medium might not be the reenergizing of values and self-discipline that made it and our country great. It is time to call junk what it is—junk, and dirt what it is—dirt, and sin what it is—sin. Self-discipline in radio might conceivably help us realize a new golden age—instead of another dark age.

Art Linkletter: The electronic media have fostered the steady disintegration of good manners, civility, and happy (Cinderella) endings. People like Howard Stern and Jerry Springer ride the crest of this wave of trash.

Dick Fatherley: Howard Stern is considered the country's top "shock" jock. There are others, too. In the case of Stern, I feel that he is in need of some professional help. His routine is tired. He's tired. His audience is tired. His radio network is failing to attract new affiliates. It is time to move on to something new and fresh. Stern is "old."

Dick Orkin: I think Stern is unique because he knows he is pushing and testing the limits—a veritable Lenny Bruce of the blue ether. And, like Bruce, he is witty and clever, and in some perverse way, he reminds us of radio's strength as an up-close and intimate medium. His power as a performer, I think, comes from the fact that he talks to two audiences: the "My Gawd, he said the word 'tits' on the air!" listeners and the audience that enjoys hearing him humorously and impishly puncture the pomposity of American puritanism and its accompanying bloated sense of self-righteousness. Come to think of it, they may both be the same audience.

Larry Gelbart. I think what Howard Stern represents is beneath contempt or comment.

Steve Allen: As for Stern, I wish him good health. I have appeared on his program in a couple of instances, some years ago, and found him pleasant-enough company. Nevertheless, I will oppose to the death what his incredible dependence on vulgarity of the grossest sort is doing to the American consciousness, of both children and adults. Unlike the social critic Lenny Bruce, who employed the weapons of wit and courageous insight in expressing himself, Stern has little to say about the conditions of life on our troubled planet. He has become enormously successful, to put the matter very simply, by "talking dirty." Absolutely nothing he says can claim the defense that at least he is making a political or moral point. It is my personal opinion that Stern himself is a hopeless case. Concerned Christians, Jews, and Muslims, who are sickened by his broadcasts, may feel they are well advised to remember him in their prayers. But more meaningful and productive criticism should be directed at those network executives and those individual station owners who, knowing full well that Mr. Stern makes a living by indulging in the most revolting forms of vulgarity and sleaze, nevertheless decide to put him on the air. Why do they do so? Certainly not because they are in personal sympathy with his depravity. There is no message that he wishes to convey that they secretly or openly agree with and therefore wish to give a platform to. Their motivation is simply the ever-popular "making a buck," which is to say that they have no sensible defense at all. And remember, as bad as the Stern radio broadcasts and telecasts are, they have served as horrible examples in that in many American cities we now find little local Howard Sterns who have evidently concluded that since being professionally disgusting has worked so well for Howard, they might as well give it a try themselves. Frighteningly, not only are they giving it a try, they are succeeding too. They are, in other words, further extrapolating Stern's morally vile "anything goes" message.

Stan Freberg: I hate the whole shock-jock thing. When I think about the censorship that I had to endure—these guys would never have existed back then. When I did *The Stan Freberg Show* on the CBS radio network, Standards and Practices was constantly hovering over me. They were surprised and unnerved by my satire. After the first show featuring a piece called "El Sodom and the Rancho Gomorra in Las Vegas," they said "Holy mackerel, we got more than we bargained for here!" In that show, they made me censor out any mention of the hydrogen bomb, which was in the original version of the sketch. It accidentally got fed to New York anyway. I recount a lot of my confrontations with network censors in my book, *It Only Hurts When I Laugh.* The censors were always saying you can't do this or you can't do that. Don't offend the Spanish people or, *oy vay,* don't insult the Jews. You could make a satirical ethnic reference to the Swiss, and that was somehow acceptable though. Go figure. It is probably my Christian upbringing that causes me to be offended and repulsed by some of the stuff that people like Howard Stern say on the air. When guys like Don Imus or Stern use the word "penis" on the air, I think back to the censorship we were subjected to and shake my head. Shock radio is a gimmick. But despite all this, I think Stern is a very funny guy, who does make people listen to the medium. I'm a great fan of Don Imus, too. He's a talented guy. Actually, Imus is a fan of mine, I'm told, so how could I dislike him?

Larry Gelbart: Stern's listeners obviously enjoy having him act out the most hateful parts of themselves, but remember, I said I'm not going to comment, right?

Walter Cronkite: They call it shock radio, but what they are basically about is hard-core pornography.

Karl Haas: Those who tune the shock jocks speak highly of them. They are out there, so if people want to listen to them, it is their prerogative. I am not going to sit in judgment of them. Besides, I don't think they do any harm.

Peter Wolf: Shock jocks like Stern have their place on the dial, and they should be allowed to be there, I think. Jesus, what is all the hubbub about anyway? Maybe the only downside is that there are just too many imitators on the air.

Steve Allen: It's a grave error to assume that fundamentalist religious believers or political conservatives are the only critics of Stern and the thousand-and-one other examples of sleaze presently so dominant in our culture. I personally take liberal or progressive positions on a good many social issues, but I don't know of any conservative who is more revolted than I am by the present sleaze-flood. I also know people all across the political and philosophical spectrum who feel as I do. It is a mistake, therefore, and a serious one, to perceive the present controversy as a conservatives versus the media formulation.

Blanquita Cullum: Whenever I am asked my opinion of Howard Stern and the myriad of other so-called "shock" jocks, all I say is that I support their freedom of speech. I leave it at that.

Larry Gelbart: As much as I detest them, I would have to say likewise. Hopefully, these guys are preaching only to the perverted. Is that another comment?

Shel Swartz: A friend and colleague of mine, the late Lee Fowler, whose last job was as a talk-radio host at WJNO in West Palm Beach, Florida, where I also worked at the time, explained to me why his own airshift was loaded with sexual innuendoes and obscenities. He said, right to my face, and I'll never forget it, "Shel, today you're either outrageous on the air, or you're out of work."

Robert Hilliard: The airwaves should be available and accessible to everybody, regardless of point of view, as long as they are not used to inspire hatred or prejudice.

Deejay liner:

Wrap your legs around the radio.

—Tom Donahue

Part IV

Into the New Millennium

19

Business by the *Book*

Impressions Count

*That action is best, which procures the greatest
happiness for the greatest numbers.*
—Francis Hutcheson

*Calvin Coolidge observed that "the business of America is business,"
to which humorist Will Rogers supposedly added, "And radio 'is'
America, so figure it out," when he was asked to comment on the
extreme commercialization of the medium.*

*Indeed, radio stations do make their living—their life-sustaining
revenues and profits—by selling "spot" time (public stations with noncommercial licenses seek corporate funding to sponsor their programs), and it is axiomatic—sayeth the advertising agency media
buyer—that for a radio operation to enjoy monetary success it must
have an audience. Ad agencies place "buys" on commercial stations
that do have the "bodies"—to use the professional lingo.*

*Most radio stations depend on services that provide them with lis-
tener statistics. Broadcasters refer to these published findings as the
"book" or the "bible"—an indication of the lofty reverence in which
they are held. Says station owner Jay Williams Jr., "Without the numbers, selling airtime becomes a hat trick of a very different nature. In
the surveyed markets (and most meaningful markets are surveyed),
your position in the ratings can make or break you. It is a fiercely
competitive environment out there." Competitive, indeed! With up-
wards of ten thousand commercial stations in the country—some cities
have fifty or more—the fight for audiences and sponsors becomes a*

very heated and complex one. Inevitably, the spoils of this battle royal go to those who have garnered a desirable numerical ranking in the latest listener survey.

Ratings companies have been around since the late 1920s. The first to provide audience data to the industry was Crossley in 1929. A few years later, Hooper, Inc. offered a similar service. Both were followed (and eventually supplanted) by other ratings companies, among them The Pulse, Nielsen, Birch, and Arbitron, which became (and remains) the preeminent tabulator of radio-audience size.

In the nineteen-eighties, Arbitron was challenged by Birch Radio, which sought to provide its subscribers with more "qualitative" data than its numerically dependent arch rival. However, by 1990, it found itself defunct, leaving the "Big A," as some broadcasters sarcastically refer to Arbitron, to dominate the radio-ratings field.

Just how important are the numbers to most radio stations? "Without the 'book' you might as well pull the plug," says prominent industry executive Norm Feuer.

Joe Cortese: Make no mistake about it, radio is a numbers-driven business in the year 2000. Stations in big markets, in particular, rely on the figures. If they fall, you can expect things to happen.

Elliot Reid: It really was no different during radio's golden age. Ratings were of central importance then too. I'm sure that stars with major series—Eve Arden, Lucy, Burns and Allen, and others—were in those boardrooms and did play a role in how radio (at least with respect to their shows) was being shaped. Of course, the point of departure of all meetings were ratings—good ones, not so good ones, the hope of good ones, or just plain "What the hell are we gonna do now with these numbers?"

Marvin Bensman: There are hundreds of research organizations engaged entirely or in part in radio, television, and cable audience research. First, one group of concerns—American Research Bureau, A.C. Nielsen, and at times others—provide regular "ratings" that serve as indices of program popularity or audience size and demographics of broadcast programs. These companies are audited and accredited by the Electronic Media Rating Council, which was formed in 1972 to prevent government regulation of rating services. Second, a number of companies —among them the Institute for Motivational Research, the Psychological Corporation, and Schwerin Research Corporation—specialize in qualitative audience research into the effectiveness of programs or of commercial announcements. There are also research organizations that provide wide-ranging information for various constituents. There are polling organizations such as Roper, Yankovich, and Gallup. There are focus group researchers studying consumers' responses to content from programs to advertising. Universities also provide specialized research as well.

Arthur C. Nielsen Jr.: Let me share with you a few observations about my company's role in the early days of audience measurement. Ratings were important in radio as they enabled advertisers and their agencies to select programs that were heard by people who were the best prospects for their goods and services. In this way they increased the efficiency of advertising, resulting in lower prices and contributing to a higher standard of living for all. Ratings also helped broadcasters develop programs of general interest with broad appeal. By 1945, the two main sources of ratings were C.E. Hooper and A.C. Nielsen. "Hooperatings" were derived from a telephone panel of households located in about thirty major cities. "Nielsen ratings" were collected from households located throughout the country, by means of a meter attached to a radio. The industry generally preferred the Hooperatings, as they could be delivered faster than the Nielsen ratings and cost less. Nielsen's major supporters were primarily large national advertisers, who could afford to pay Nielsen's higher price. They realized that, although slower in delivery than Hooperatings, Neilsen provided a more accurate estimate of listening throughout the entire country. The Nielsen figures revealed that many people in smaller towns and rural areas preferred somewhat different programs from those favored by people living in the larger cities. The Hooper data collection method did not lend itself to providing a true national sample. Covering the entire country would have required their making a large number of long-distance, high-cost phone calls. Furthermore, frequent calling of households in small towns proved to be annoying to responders, resulting in unacceptably low cooperation levels. The major metropolitan areas—the areas where Hooper made their measurements—were the first to receive television broadcasts. Many medium-sized towns had only one station, and a large part of the country at that time had no TV coverage at all. The result was that Hooper's measurements dramatically underestimated the overall radio audiences, since listening remained largely unaffected in much of the country where TV broadcasts were unavailable. It became readily apparent that the Nielsen method had been a more accurate technique for many years, although it was virtually impossible for Nielsen to demonstrate this fact because there is no empirical way of determining how many people listen to a radio signal sent out across the airways. As a consequence of the now-revealed shortcomings in his ratings, Mr. Hooper's business became unprofitable and was sold to A.C. Nielsen, which used the increased income to enlarge its radio-sample sizes as well as to modify its equipment in order to measure television. Around this time two important developments took place that profoundly affected radio. One was the invention of the transistor by scientists at Bell Laboratory, and the other was the passage of mass-highway-construction legislation. The transistor, when built into small, low-cost portable radios, increased out-of-home listening. The expanded highway program had the same effect as people and businesses moved out of cities into lower-cost areas. The car radio made long commutes more pleasant. These two developments combined to make it more difficult for Nielsen to measure the entire radio audience as out-of-home listening continued to grow and Nielsen's meter measured only in-home listening to nonportable sets. In addition, the government's policy of licensing more radio stations divided up the available audience, making it more difficult to measure programs accurately—particularly those with low ratings—on both AM and FM. The Nielsen team made a real effort to modify its methods so as to provide useful research on the radio audience under the changing conditions. We developed three proposals of differing quality and cost, all requiring larger expenditures for the research. My father presented them in New York City to a large group of radio executives, agency representatives, and advertisers. After the presentation, it was obvious that there was little industry support, even for the least comprehensive and expensive system. As the shortcomings of the radio ratings became more apparent, the A.C. Nielsen Company was subjected to criticism that was difficult to take. My father and his associates felt that the broadcast industry, which was quite profitable, should bear the cost of the necessary changes. Unfortunately, it appeared that it was more interested, at the time, in the future of television and so was unwilling to bear the added costs of improving radio ratings. With considerable reluctance, the company decided to discontinue its radio-measurement service and directed its attention to improving its television-ratings service. It seemed to offer better commercial returns. As a postscript, it may be of interest to know that the company spent twenty-eight years in an effort to provide reliable audience measurements of radio listening. The effort began in 1936 when the company took over a patent obtained by Professor Woodruff of MIT for an instrument designed to record radio listening. While solid in concept, the meter proved to be unreliable and impractical in commercial application. The next ten years were spent developing decoding devices, systems for lowering costs, speeding up delivery of reports, and simplifying the analysis of data. The service known as the Nielsen Radio Index was launched in 1946. The first ratings reports were delivered eleven weeks after the broadcast. Continuing research over many years eventually made it possible to deliver ratings overnight. In order to accomplish these service improvements, more than one hundred patents were obtained by A.C. Nielsen Company—all developed by Nielsen employees in the company's own laboratory. In spite of this effort, the A.C. Nielsen Company never made a profit on its radio-ratings service. In fact, the company lost money for seventeen years. While the company was best known for its radio- and television-ratings service, it never amounted to more than ten percent of the company's total revenue.

Christopher Sterling: The appearance of Nielsen ratings for television and Arbitron for radio eliminated the long-standing Hooperatings. Its telephone survey approach was supplanted by meters and diaries, both proving more efficient.

Dave Archard: The Hooperatings were really the key measurement service into the fifties. Hooper hired local people to make telephone calls to measure local radio listenership. Since the first question by the Hooper caller was "Were you listening to the radio when the phone rang?" some enterprising station programmers (I'm thinking of a guy named Roy Nilson) created a simple contest that went something like this: "When your phone rings, answer it by saying 'I'm listening to the new WALT Radio.' If it's us calling, you'll win eleven dollars and ten cents" (the station's frequency—1110-AM). Needless to say, this the Hooper caller's job easier. I once did a top-forty countdown show on Saturday afternoons that grabbed a fifty-two share in Hooper—a record that I don't believe has ever been broken. In the sixties, WTSP in St. Petersburg, airing a dreadful mix of music and Mutual programs, decided to go top forty. They hired Roy Nilson away from WALT just prior to my being fired. Nilson hired me after I experienced several weeks of unemployment. The rest is history, as the call letters were changed to WLCY ("Elsie"), the signal was full time (compared to WALT's daytime drawback), and a larger audience was attracted. The Pulse Rating Service entered the market, and soon it was: "Pulse and Hooper agree! WLCY is Number One on Great Tampa Bay!"

Peter Orlik: Radio became a more documentable local advertising buy in the sixties. Beginning with a 1964 study in the Detroit market, Arbitron expanded its use of personal diaries to measure listeners into fifteen markets by 1966. By 1971, it was providing its local listenership measurement service in one hundred fifty markets.

James Fletcher: An event of no small importance in broadcasting during the nineteen-sixties was the disappearance of the A.C. Nielsen Company from the radio-ratings field. Mr. Nielsen Sr.—partly in response to the annoyance of the congressional hearings on the ratings—proposed an "honest and adequate" rating system for the medium, which broadcasters were unwilling to pay for. The field of radio ratings was left to Arbitron, despite the fact that very few stations actually subscribed to full-service coverage.

Marlin Taylor: Arbitron and Pulse surveys were not the only way of measuring listening, especially in small markets. I used to tell my people that the amount of times a client's cash register rings is another very good barometer of audience size.

Ed Shane: The audience measurement challenge intensified in the nineteen-seventies. Christopher Lasch's *Culture of Narcissism* played itself out in the general culture and found a parallel in response to radio. It wasn't enough to have radio that was specifically for one generation. Now each subgroup by age and lifestyle found its own sound, its own reflection of self. Alvin Toffler introduced us to the word "demassification" in 1980 with the publication of his *The Third*

Wave. "An information bomb is exploding in our midst," he wrote, "showering us with a shrapnel of images and drastically changing the way each of us perceives and acts upon our private world." He was one of only a few who could see where radio—where media—was going. The "mind-model of reality," as Toffler put it, "is unique to each of us." "Me" became more important than "us." The power of video magnified "me" far beyond what radio could do. HBO, CNN, and MTV defined specificity for viewers twenty-four hours a day. Others came on their heels, thanks to satellite technology. Choice proliferated. Radio remained a "mass" medium, especially when compared to cable channels. Listeners wanted greater choice from their radio, but radio needed audiences large enough to sell to advertisers. So listeners began to "mix and match" their radio options—news, traffic, and Paul Harvey from one station, country music from another. Lite favorites from one station, "the clunk joke of the day" from another. Measuring all this was a complex undertaking.

Pierre Bouvard: In response to this in recent years, Arbitron has deepened its research efforts and services manifold times. For example, recently we completed an exhaustive national study of three thousand Americans in which we probed the use of the Internet and interest in other new technologies. Interestingly, when we asked participants what types of information they would be most interested in seeing on radio-station Web sites, they rated local information highest.

Joe Cortese: Radio has become so overresearched that spontaneity no longer exists. The "stats" are what count—they are a way of life. It has become so rigid on the air.

Robert Hilliard: What ratings reflect the most is how programming to the lowest common denominator can be so successful in just garnering numbers and not minds. Just think about what "number one" means today.

Blanquita Cullum: Radio ratings matter as far as money is concerned, but they don't necessarily measure quality. They really have less to do with quality and more to do with hype.

Howard K. Smith: The fixation on ratings has directly impacted programming quality. Anyone can deduce that fact.

Dick Orkin: Do you know how many really good things have fallen victim to the numbers game? To me the great mystery of this broadcast century may be why people like talk-host Michael Jackson of KABC were taken off the air. You can be sure his removal was driven by audience numbers and therefore was an economic decision. Yet it still remains a baffling mystery. I guess it is made all the more so by the fact that it happened in an enlightened, modern-marketing era of "keep and develop" the existing share of the *audience* as opposed to growing an increased share of the *market*. It happened in a broadcast medium that touts the economic and reach advantages of target or niche-directed advertising. Just when you think you got it all figured out . . . ha!

Sign-off:

Bye, bye, Kemo Sabe!

—Dan Ingram

20

Going Public

Noncommercial Radio

*Though the Philistines may jostle, you will rank
as an apostle in the high aesthetic band.*

—W.S. Gilbert

*The two things that contributed most to the creation of public radio in
America were the general lack of programming diversity and depth in the
medium and its commercial clutter. It was because of the widespread
dissatisfaction with existing radio that National Public Radio, with financial support from the Corporation for Public Broadcasting, was launched
in 1970. Less than a dozen years later American Public Radio (eventually
Public Radio International) joined NPR in providing what former CBS
newswriter and producer Ed Bliss called "The most profuse, varied, and
informative programming heard anywhere."*[1]

*Today, millions of radio listeners tune public radio's award-
winning programs, among them* All Things Considered, Morning Edition, Fresh Air, A Prairie Home Companion, Car Talk, This American
Life, *and* Says You, *to mention a scant few. However, despite its
popular and critical success, it has not been without its detractors.*

*In the mid-1990s, a mostly Republican Congress roundly assailed
public broadcasting for what Congress perceived as "liberal bias and
began efforts to reduce and eventually eliminate funding of the service.
Today, most public radio stations rely on corporate underwriters and
listener contributions to keep themselves afloat. So far, so good, but
the future of the medium is fraught with financial uncertainty, although its fan base continues to expand.*

Sam Sauls: The FCC's allocation after the war of twenty FM channels set aside exclusively for noncommercial use (between 88.1 and 91.9 megahertz) really anticipated public radio. Certainly the growth of educational FM radio, generally the staple of college and university stations, can be attributed to this allocation.

Christopher Sterling: Jump ahead to the Carnegie Commission in 1967 providing a blueprint for the conversion of educational to public broadcasting, and there you have it.

Sam Sauls: From this came the Public Broadcasting Act and the Corporation for Public Broadcasting. The latter is a private, nonprofit corporation designed to oversee the distribution of the annual federal contribution to the national public broadcasting system. In addition to funding diverse radio and television programming, CPB also distributes grants to CPB-supported public radio and TV stations throughout the United States and its territories. CPB created the Public Broadcasting Service (PBS) for television in 1969 and National Public Radio (NPR) in 1970.

Charles Howell: NPR was created as a fresh and innovative alternative to what was on the airwaves.

Ed Shane: Exactly, and you know most listeners discovered public radio by turning the dial looking for something they couldn't get from their local commercial outlets. Not long after *Car Talk* began on NPR stations, I was hearing Click and Clack in focus groups in cities all over the country. Garrison Keillor's *Prairie Home Companion* showed the same pattern of grassroots discovery. A listener in New Orleans told me of tuning away from WWL's morning news each day to hear a voice actor's character telling a story on a public station in Vicksburg, Mississippi.

Charles Howell: The original mission statement for NPR offers a glimpse of how the network's founders first conceptualized the idea of NPR. It stated that it served the individual, promoted personal growth, respected differences among men, and "celebrated the human experience as infinitely varied rather than vacuous and banal." William Siemering, NPR's cofounder and program director, fused this poetic declaration into something that made NPR a very different radio service from what had existed up to that time. NPR was not to be some top-down network service. Entertainment was not the only goal, but also programs to help promote enlightened human understanding.

William Siemering: Noncommercial radio is as old as radio itself in the United States. The first continuous broadcast station was WHA at the University of Wisconsin in Madison. There this new invention fit well with the university's motto: "The boundaries of the campus are the boundaries of the state." We do well to recall the idea behind the development of public broadcasting, which was to promote the populist ideals of extending knowledge and culture to as many people as possible, not unlike the free public library. Early on, the commercial networks took this mission seriously as well. CBS had a schedule of in-school programs, and NBC supported a symphony orchestra under the baton of Arturo Toscanini. As commercial radio moved down a more pop-culture path, educational radio retained its serious mission and the programming was proper, dignified, earnest, and, yes, sometimes dull. Some of the most popular programs were fifty-minute lectures and half-hour readings from contemporary fiction. Stations exchanged programs via a tape network, and there was no live interconnection. The passage of the Public Broadcasting Act of 1967 forced us to drop the name "educational" for the more inclusive and broader "public" broadcasting. That suited many of us who were regarded as young Turks. Our vision came both from what we saw as the weaknesses of commercial radio and from the imperative to reflect the pluralism of America. The anger, urgency, and (unfortunately) the moral tone of superiority are captured in an article I wrote in 1969. Allow me to quote from it, and pardon my doing so:

> Thus far the media have presented the world from a single perspective, and they have viewed political and social minorities as a spectator views animals in a cage.
>
> Racism and hate will not disappear with more high-rise apartments or larger police forces, but through meaningful communication. Integration of diverse ideas within the media must accompany an integrated society.
>
> Ignorance resulting in fear, hate, and suppression has been allowed to grow out of neglect. If we are to be true to our name and high hopes,

we must provide a program service meeting human needs—esthetic, intellectual and affective. Rather than a mass medium which tries to unite us in a common banality, public broadcasting must unite us in our common humanity.

These ideas did not originate in an ivory tower. Network news at the time was the white-male authority in New York. Many of us had smelled the acrid smoke of burning buildings, seen neighborhood stores looted and the windows covered with dull plywood. Our eyes were burned by tear gas. We heard and saw how urban and campus demonstrations were reported in terms of the damage to property rather than looking at the underlying causes. The anger at not being heard could not be contained. It raged through the ghettos to college campuses. Since most white images of blacks came from pictures of demonstrations or of criminals being led to court in handcuffs, I wanted to counter that by establishing a community broadcast center in the heart of the black community in Buffalo, New York. As manager WBFO-FM, the radio station of the State University of New York at Buffalo, I sought to enable these residents to plan and produce twenty-five hours a week of programming. We sponsored a black arts festival, where listeners—black and white—could hear poetry, music, and stories, as well as broadcasts of issues and concerns. When I was asked to write the original mission statement for National Public Radio in 1970, this is what I came up with:

NPR will regard individual differences with respect and joy rather than derision and hate. It will celebrate the human experience as infinitely varied rather than vacuous and banal. It will encourage a sense of active constructive participation, rather than apathetic helplessness.

NPR will not substitute superficial blandness for genuine diversity of regions, values, cultural and ethnic minorities which comprise American society. It will speak with many voices and many dialects.

In other words, we were no longer content to define public radio as simply noncommercial, as a passive transmitter of culture, but rather as something to be engaged with the most critical issues of contemporary life; something to strengthen democracy itself—lofty as that sounds. For the first time the public radio stations were linked by telephone lines so we could capitalize on the immediacy of the medium. The first feed from NPR was the Senate Foreign Relations Committee hearings on Vietnam in April 1971. We launched the news and information program *All Things Considered* on May third of that year. It aired at five P.M. and was intended to be the first and most comprehensive presentation of the day's events. We never wanted NPR to be regarded as an "alternative" service. In order to broaden its appeal, we employed a conversational style to distinguish it from commercial radio and the elite, often British, sound of much of public television at the time. We wanted to get out of the studio, to use natural sound to help tell the stories—a kind of photojournalism for the ear. We wanted to use the individual stations as a source of stories. We considered the work of artists and writers to be of equal importance to that of politicians and included it as part of the day's events. As the title stated, we considered *all* things. Of course, turning these ideals into realities wasn't an easy chore. The early programs could be both brilliant and awful. In a meeting that took place shortly before we began, station managers were very critical of our plan. They expected something that would be the equivalent of CBS. Women, some said, lacked authority, and their voices transmitted poorly. Despite this, we stuck it out and worked to improve our craft and editorial edge. Now NPR is generally regarded as the best source of news and information on radio, and it has replaced CBS in that regard. It is listened to widely by professional journalists, decision makers, and public officials. In spite of all the new sources of information, public radio occupies a unique role in American life. The vision has been made real.

Charles Howell: Pacifica radio also occupies a unique place in the panoply of American radio broadcasting. According to writer Ralph Engelman's overview of noncommercial radio *(Public Radio and Television in America),* Pacifica has long stood as a force for independence and opposition to commercial broadcasters, while NPR has slowly become more and more of an organ the commercial broadcasters use to opt out of any responsibility for delivering upon their obligations of preserving the public "interest, convenience, and necessity."

Yuri Rasovsky: I guess I'll provide the voice of dissent in this discussion. Sorry, but I have a very low opinion of public radio. It seems to me that it is a permanently fatuous industry that has blown most of its opportunities. By and large it has given up its role as a medium of artistic expression, leaving practitioners such as myself pretty much out in the cold. Public radio has never come to grips with its mission; the subject necessarily comes up at every conclave and is invariably tabled. There is no overview. Political wrangling, complacency, incompetence, opportunism, philistinism, and just plain laziness are endemic on the management side. The people who control the airtime are woefully out of touch with listeners and, therefore, in a perpetual state of panic over what to do to get listener contributions. The three interrelated, equally important communities of public radio—the networks, the stations, and the producers—treat each other with the greatest contempt. How the public is served by this and the concomitant degradation of programming is a mystery.

Douglas Gomery: Over the years critics have argued that NPR executives have tried to mediate the widely varied concerns of member station managers by adopting "quasi-commercial" programming strategies.

Dick Fatherley: Allow me to join the ranks of those critical of public broadcasting. These government-subsidized radio stations have no business on the broadcast bands. They hold no economic interest in their audiences because their programming is not created to attract tune-in or to maintain marketable average quarter-hour audiences for sale to advertisers. Instead, NPR and PBS are a panhandling, government-underwritten public address system for kid-gloved, silk-stocking ideologists.

Douglas Gomery: Public broadcasting's critics have included those within the government itself. For example, President Nixon sought to crush what he perceived as this upstart liberal tool, this alternative news source. His threats against the medium subsided as the Watergate scandal heated up.

Frank Tavares: When Ronald Reagan took office in January 1981, one of the agendas of his new administration was to eliminate public broadcasting. Even with "forward funding," a concept that protected public broadcasting from political congressional whims by providing its budget two years in advance, things took an ugly turn. Budgets were slashed in anticipation. At NPR, we had just begun to pursue new money-making ventures in technological partnerships with commercial companies. But new ventures required expansion and investment, something that became increasingly difficult. Toward the end of 1982, serious financial straits forced NPR to jettison its new ventures and cut back drastically. It didn't help. By the middle of the next year, a third of the staff had been laid off, and there were serious doubts that the network would survive. An interim management team devised an emergency financial rescue with the help of the Corporation for Public Broadcasting. The price of the plan would forever change the way public radio was funded in the United States and, in doing so, make NPR and other public radio suppliers more directly responsible to the needs of stations and listeners than ever before. Ultimately, what it meant for domestic public radio was a new focus on the audience. NPR's goal was to double its audience throughout the decade. Public radio audience research—primarily that of David Giovannoni—broke new ground. The mission of public radio remained constant, but new programming strategies added millions of listeners. Public radio's curse of the nineteen-eighties has shown itself to be a blessing. The change in funding strategies, although anathema to many, has made noncommercial radio in this country stronger and more effective in reaching listeners than it has ever been.

Sam Sauls: You might say public broadcasting's difficulty has a sort of boomerang-effect history, because in the mid-nineteen-nineties the federal funding of CPB was under congressional scrutiny. At stake again was the possible reduction of federal funding whose impact would certainly be felt on public radio programming.

Newton Minow: Despite all the rumblings, there was improvement and growth in public radio in the nineteen-eighties, while interestingly there was a decline of commercial-radio public-service obligations.

LeRoy Bannerman: I don't think it can be pointed out often enough that, in recent decades, NPR has added an important dimension to radio's role in contemporary society. While developing a new concept in news, it has also expanded the medium's creative parameters in documentary and drama.

Steve Allen: The best radio stations of all are those in the public-radio sector. Indeed, an unbiased listener—if there is any such thing—may find it hard to believe the public radio stations and far too many commercial stations are appealing to the same human race. The public stations daily provide fare of such a high-minded, uplifting, and admirable sort that the judgmental mind is somewhat unsettled. Its speakers address us grammatically, coherently, and reasonably. There is no hysteria, no paranoia, no disregard for such ancient admonitions as, for example, "Thou shalt not bear false witness against thy neighbor." The price paid by public radio, of course, for such admirable professional conduct is low ratings. On hundreds of commercial stations, by way of depressing contrast, we see a shameful overload of commercials, a frenetic rush-rush of sensory impressions, (evidently based on the general perception that the average American listener now has the attention span of a gnat), and an astonishing lack of interest in assorted standards and values.

Peter Wolf: Public radio is the only place you get diversity today. I listen for the great variety it provides. In my opinion, it certainly is not a waste of tax dollars.

Stan Freberg: National Public Radio is doing something very worthwhile. It's an oasis of stimulating programming in a bland commercial desert.

Susan Stamberg: Forgive my public radio chauvinism, but I would have to agree and add that today, as the commercial television networks merge themselves out of straight news reporting, NPR has become the primary news source for millions and millions of people in this country and abroad.

Howard K. Smith: I think public radio news does a commendable job and is quite good. This is the kind of radio I listen to when I can. It can be a very rewarding experience.

Frank Tavares: Of course, I suppose I too could be accused of bias, having spent so much of my professional life at NPR, but I truly believe the establishment of public radio changed the face of American broadcasting. It consciously took up the mantle laid down by many icons of news and information broadcasting—Edward R. Murrow himself, among others. It searched for ways of gathering and distributing news, information, and performance programming that had not been possible among noncommercial stations previously. I began my tenure at NPR in 1978. During my first week on the job, I was seated at a dinner table with several of my colleagues listening to the network's relatively new president, Frank Mankiewicz, deliver a speech. On my right was the network's new vice president of distribution, Billy Oxley. We had started work on the same day and were sharing plans. Oxley's primary responsibility was to get NPR's satellite distribution system up and running. His goal was simple—give any news producer the ability to pick up the phone, dial a single number, and order up a satellite channel for his or her programming needs. Sounds simple today, but in September 1972, it was just a vision.

Norman Corwin: Alas, government will never underwrite big bucks for radio, and neither will commercial broadcasting. Today the only entity that might hustle to carry Archibald MacLeish's type of program is public radio, always high-minded but perpetually poor alongside conglomerates owned by industrial behemoths like General Electric and Westinghouse. National Public Radio and Public Radio International (formerly American Public Radio) will continue to be what they are now—a brave minority subsisting on what, in respectable financial circles, is loose change. The only chance for a renaissance of the kind of radio that MacLeish, John Dunning, this writer, and cabalists who share our outlook believe in would be if some benign Croesus like Ted Turner, the splendid maverick who donated a billion dollars to a needy United Nations, took an interest in the subject. Such an almsgiver could outfit production and underwrite a year's public radio network time for considerably less than the single-season wage of a star baseball pitcher.

Note

1. Ed Bliss, *Now the News: The Story of Broadcast Journalism* (New York: Columbia University Press, 1991), p. 195.

Sign-off:

So long from Lake Wobegon where all the women are strong, all the men are good looking, and all the children are above average.
—Garrison Keillor

21

Turn of the Screw

Tubes and Wires in a Box

> With the fairy tales of science, and the long
> result of time.
>
> —Lord Tennyson

Radio is more than the utterances manufactured by mere mortals. It is technology—equipment, studios, transmitters, and antennas. Without the electronic devices and mechanisms designed to process the flow of audio (the hoots and brays of human discourse) and the engineers who operate these "whatchamacallit-thingamajigs," as many "nontech" types (on-air personalities, for instance) call them, there would be no radio medium. It is first a science and then—if the muses prevail—an art.

Since World War II, many technological innovations have contributed to the making of modern-day radio. The list includes, among so many other things, the transistor, which gave the medium greater mobility and portability; the car radio, which provided the medium with its new prime-time audience; the studio cartridge, which made things easier and more efficient for deejays; stereo processing, which brought more listeners to the FM band; automation systems, which reduced operating expenditures; digital recordings, which sharpened station fidelity; "smart" receiver technology, which finally gave radio the visual component it longed for; and so forth.

As much as anything else, it has been the efforts of audio technologists and engineers that have kept the medium relevant since the invasion of television all the way up to the era of today's information superhighway. Talk-show hosts and disc jockeys did not participate in

the creation and development of the "wireless" communication appa-
ratus. Those who did were men of science and technology—Marconi,
DeForest, Armstrong, Fleming, Fessenden, and a host of others (we
dare not forget to mention Tesla, as his devotees are most zealous in
their mission to accord him recognition)—and these extraordinary in-
dividuals stood on the shoulders of earlier inventors and experiment-
ers of the electromagnetic realm.

Ed Bliss: It is impossible to think of radio without seeing it in a
technological context. At CBS News shortly after the war, I was witness to the arrival of audio tape and the gratification of those who had
been working with the old disks and magnetized steel wire. On rare
occasions wire recorders were used, with dramatic results, by radio
correspondents during the war. (Notably by George Hicks of ABC
News on D-Day and Edward R. Murrow of CBS News during the
Battle of Britain.) Wire was faulty because it tended to twist and was
difficult to edit. Paper tape coated with iron oxide was easier to edit
but likely to break. I remember well the old brush recorder used at
CBS and how recorded programs were played from two machines in
case the tape on one should snap. Finally I.G. Farben developed the
coated plastic tape that is used today. I celebrate the development of
magnetic recording, which enabled radio audiences to hear the voices
and natural sounds of history.

Robert Hilliard: Unfortunately, it took technology a while to reach
the hinterlands. Although the tape recorder had been developed in the
United States from the German prototypes captured at the end of the
war, not too many stations were using it. For example, in 1953 I wrote,
produced, and directed a series called *The Delaware Story*—a state of
Delaware version of *The Ohio Story*—on radio station WDEL in Wilmington. These half-hour historical docudramas were recorded for
later playback on the disc-cutting machine. I recall the frustration of
reaching the fifteen-minute or even twenty-nine-minute mark when
someone fluffed a line or the sound-effects person missed a cue and
we had to start again from the top. That happened too frequently, so it
was good to see the arrival of audio tape.

Irving Fang: Also toward the end of this period transistors were going
into radios in place of tubes, making radio sets smaller and more

durable. Portable radios were carried to the beach and radios were built into cars. People could even listen to radio programs at the drive-in movie theaters that were springing up everywhere, especially near the new tract homes in the suburbs.

Robert Mounty: The innovation and market introduction of the transistor was one of the most positive things to happen to radio on the heels of TV's debut.

Christopher Sterling: Very true. The transistor's appearance in the form of the legitimately portable radio increased the medium's popularity at a time when it needed a boost.

Jack Brown: The miniaturization of sets that transistors made possible gave the medium a new lease on life by attracting the young audience it needed to help reverse its declining fortunes.

Marvin Bensman: In spite of the increasingly dominant position of television, purchase of radio sets, especially of portable and transistor sets, continued heavy. The first mass-market transistor "pocket" radio was introduced in 1954 and sold for forty-nine ninety-five. AM-set sales in 1952 were ten million; in 1955, fifteen million; in 1965, twenty million. Auto-set sales went from three million in 1952 to ten million by 1965 for a total of forty-two million auto sets in use by 1965. Estimates are that from 1957 or 1958, nearly ninety-eight percent of all homes were radio-equipped.

Mary Ann Watson: Our transistors went everywhere with us—on the walk to the library, to the bus stop, window shopping, even to bed at night. It seemed only natural that each day should have a continuous sound track of popular music. In the early nineteen-sixties we were eager to assimilate into a wider American culture, and our miniature radios were the passports. While our grandparents listened to news about the old country, we sang along to the top-forty records and commercial jingles and schemed to meet our favorite disc jockeys. These little sets weren't built for durability though. Scotch tape could hold a cracked piece of plastic for only so long. Before the owner finished high school, the transistor was demoted from gem to junk. God only knows how many transistor radios have been unceremoniously pitched—each one a player in someone's uniquely American coming-of-age story.

Frank Tavares: The portability of radio receivers, made possible by the production of cheap transistors, was a major factor in the evolution of the medium. Although portable radios had been available much earlier, they required large, heavy, expensive batteries. The cheap transistor radio freed the listener from the console in the living room, the table model in the kitchen, and the dashboard receiver in the car. It was easy to take the medium any place. This was significant, as television receivers were stationary. Viewers had to gather around them as listeners had once done with radio consoles. The portability of radio was something television could not replicate. It gave the medium a distinct uniqueness. In this respect, radio always had the advantage over television. Portable audio-recording equipment appeared years before practical video recorders. And analog-audio-tape editing was quick and possible in the studio or the field. Delivering the audio from site to transmitter had always been easier than video, too. In a pinch, any phone line, regardless of fidelity, could be used to transfer a usable signal for a news report.

Ed Shane: So many of these innovations and changes were a result of the newly attained world peace following years of war. Technology—turning to peaceful production after years of feeding the engines of war—brought several wonders. One was the thirty-three-and-a-third-rpm album, another was the forty-five–rpm single. They made music radio possible.

Frank Tavares: Ahead there were to be many additional technological advances in radio. In the studio, as a producer and on-air personality, I found the appearance of the continuous-loop, self-cueing audio-cartridge machine revolutionary. At local stations, many of us operated our own control "boards" as we broadcast. At these "combo" operations, we cued the tapes, cued the records, read the advertising copy, and read the news without the help of an in-studio engineer or producer. The "cart" allowed instant cueing of prerecorded commercials, features, sound effects, theme music, and news reports. Some stations—those that could afford the extra carts—actually started to dub the majority of the music played on the air. The technology allowed one pair of hands to do the work of two or three. It affected the pacing of the programming and gave the on-air personality more autonomy. In some cases, the technology also encouraged shortcuts that preempted the advantages. In one small station where I worked, the sales staff often recorded their own commercials for clients. Recording a series of commercials directly to a cart seemed a time saver, as long as it was done in one take. But often that didn't happen, and the retakes would make it to the air.

Robert Mounty: The introduction of stereo technology in radio had a very transforming impact on FM. Just how much stereo energized this medium can't be fully expressed.

Frank Tavares: Stereo contributed to the broader use of automated systems for operating a station. The idea that a station could virtually run on its own appeared to be a real opportunity to some, especially those programming FM outlets. For years I heard stories of jerry-rigged contraptions that station techs would devise to free an operator. In one case, a story involved a jukebox set up to play records through the night so the owner-operator could go home. It actually worked for a while until early one morning a record got stuck. That was one of the legendary tales of early experimentation, but suddenly it was real. Advances in audio technology had made it possible. New playback units could stack audio carts and play them in a prearranged order. Silent cue tones could trip reel-to-reel tape playback machines as well. The AM/FM station where I worked used this approach for their evening FM programming, allowing the two stations to be manned by a single on-air talent. And much of the time it actually worked. There were four large-capacity, reel-to-reel, rack-mounted playback decks. Three contained music that featured silent cue tones that preceded and followed each selection. One deck contained the announcing tracks, all recorded earlier in the day, and each track was followed by a cue tone for a specific machine. Prerecorded commercials and breaks were on a large cartridge carousel that held dozens of tapes. These, too, were cued by the announcer tape. The system was not exact, and the timing was not precise, however. By the end of an hour, there were no guarantees that the announcer intros and the music would match. To cover that inevitability, uninterrupted music was always played the last fifteen minutes, and at the top of the hour the equipment would cut a station break and a fresh introduction. It was a crude mechanical system, and the promise of the automated station was often overshadowed by its problems. In the AM control room, we had several alarms that warned of dead air on the FM, and those of us baby-sitting the automated station while running the live AM show often had one earphone plugged into the FM line so we could manually override any cue failures. The technology didn't quite live up to its promise. But ultimately that promise was met. Not too long ago I was visiting with a program-director friend who demonstrated how he digitally records days of programming in advance—complete with all music and announcer tracks, PSAs, and breaks to the network for news—on computer.

Marvin Bensman: The growth of computerization in broadcasting, as in business generally, has been phenomenal. A number of firms introduced the computer into the radio industry for use by networks and stations to control their daily business operations, from logging programs to handling commercial availabilities and billing.

James Fletcher: The computerization of audio production has produced the best sounds radio has ever broadcast.

Sam Sauls: Computer technology made swift advances in radio application. At about the same time, satellite programming was developed offering menus from specials to short-form drops to full-service twenty-four-hour formats. This made it possible for small- and medium-market stations to have a "big market" sound while concentrating on their most important challenge—local sales and promotion.

Bruce Mims: Significant technological advances in the 1980s include the shift of networks away from landline delivery toward satellite interconnection.

Marvin Bensman: The FCC's deregulation of satellite application led to this interconnection of the networks. It obviously was an important ruling, which had significant ramifications for the medium. Noncommercial NPR and PBS were the first to distribute by satellite to broadcast stations. The networks switched over to satellite during the early nineteen-eighties. There was a delay because the nets were afraid that, if they changed to satellite distribution, AT&T would dismantle their switching arrangements and elaborate networks that had been carefully developed over the years. If that happened, then occasional (special and backup) emergency circuits might not be so readily available. Another reason for the delay was that the nets had less to gain costwise. For one thing, transmission costs were a smaller percentage of their total costs. For another, their rates from AT&T were more favorable as the competition was recognized. At the present time, all the radio networks, as well as both AP and UPI audio news, are using satellite circuits between the east and west coasts. These are basically "trunking" circuits—the kind of usage that was envisioned when satellites first came on the scene. What is more interesting is the use of satellites as a method of distributing radio programs from syndication companies directly to stations. All radio networks have now gone to satellite distribution.

Frank Tavares: Indeed, some of the most important technological advances in broadcasting in the 1970s were developed by the people in public broadcasting—both in radio and television. Cheap, reliable satellite distribution was the most important. NPR's terrestrial system of distribution was reliable, but the further its audio signal traveled over landlines from its point of origin (Washington, D.C.), the more the quality degenerated. Those listening on the west coast heard a thin, telephone-like signal. It was adequate for news programming, but high-fidelity and stereo performance programs had to be distributed by tape. Oddly enough, for news that familiar, distant-sounding report carried a certain credibility among listeners. This is what network news was supposed to sound like. It's how it had sounded for forty years. Satellite technology changed this. Soon the satellite system was in place, and the quality of the signal was astounding. In one network planning meeting, where we were reviewing some preliminary tests, a participant actually suggested that we initially "dirty up the signal" so listeners on the west coast wouldn't doubt it was a legitimate east-coast broadcast—we didn't. The satellite system was revolutionary. Within several years, all of our commercial radio brethren had switched to satellite distribution also. They had let NPR break the ground. Actually, in the beginning, most of the commercial satellite programs were carried on NPR's satellite.

Dave Archard: Technology gave air people the gadgets—the bells and whistles—to make their shows more entertaining. To spice up the news (done by our deejays) our engineer rigged up an echo chamber and filter microphone. The dateline ("Tampa!") was done in echo followed by a headline grabber on filter ("Store hit by masked gunman!"), then into the story at breakneck speed. One day, in my lightning delivery, I had a victim "hot by a shitgun blast." I kept going. The phone never rang.

Marvin Bensman:
All of this, of course, was a boon to electronic-equipment manufacturers. No estimate is available as to how much the industry spends on such apparatus, but the total must be high. Such companies as General Electric and Westinghouse are outstanding—but there are literally scores of others from Ampex—makers of tape recorders—to Minnesota Mining—maker of audio and video tape—to the tower companies that erect transmitter antennae.

Peter Wolf: There's new product—new audio technology—surfacing every day. It works for radio and it works against it by creating distractions for listeners. That is, things like CD players and so on take part of the audience away from the medium. Even the car phone has impacted listening. So what technology gives, technology takes.

John Kittross: Yeah, but I have a feeling it gives more than takes. Have you noticed the explosion in the number of portable "boom boxes" that have been out there since the nineteen-eighties?

Frank Tavares: Technology gave birth to radio. It has been the key to its long existence, and with the Internet and webcasting it is certain to be as much of an influence in the medium's future.

Deejay liner:

Zap! You've been Morganized.

—Robert W. Morgan

22

Hoarding the Air

Stations in the Fold

The best thing we can do is make wherever
we're lost in look as much like home
as possible.

—Christopher Fry

American radio is most frequently characterized, if not defined, as a "local" medium. That is the view and position held by the National Association of Broadcasters and other broadcast organizations that fervently argue against such national services as those offered by digital satellite ("nonterrestrial") communication companies. No other country in the world can boast as many land-based ("terrestrial") radio stations so generously sprinkled across its landscape as can the United States. It is this fact, claim broadcasters, that makes it a genuine community ("people's") medium—one that neatly resonates with the democratic ideals and precepts upon which the nation is founded. Says NAB president Eddie Fritts, "Local radio is important in the life of America."

On the other hand, while radio operators wave the banner of "localism," concerns have mounted about the rampant mergers and consolidations inspired by the Telecommunications Act of 1996, wherein companies were given the opportunity to acquire unlimited numbers of stations. In just a dozen years, the total number of stations a licensee may own went from a couple dozen to several hundred.

Critics claim that this will ultimately have the effect of reducing programming diversity by engendering redundancy and sameness across the radio dial. Thus, argue critics of this trend, it will approximate the impact of those satellite services that broadcasters so vociferously argue will "genericize" the medium by altering its endemic character.

Paul Hedberg: Radio has been a local medium since before the war, really. If you examine FCC records you'll find that most communities with a population of thirty to fifty thousand population had one or two stations back then. These outlets were primarily on what the FCC deemed local-service channels—Class IV AM stations with a full-time power of two hundred fifty watts. (This power was increased to one thousand watts during the nineteen-seventies.) These local frequencies were all above twelve hundred on the AM dial. In addition to local channels, there were several regional frequencies with power between five and ten thousand watts. So the idea of radio as a local service has existed for a very long time.

Peter Orlik: Enhancing the concept of local-community service was the 1946 release of the FCC's "Public Service Responsibility of Broadcast Licensees" (later dubbed the "Blue Book"). It documented rampant overcommercialization of the industry and raised the promise-versus-performance issue to the point at which more broadcasters realized they would be held more accountable for promises made at license-renewal time. From this time on, it became clear that FCC scrutiny of a station's record would extend beyond a strictly engineering assessment of its technical operations.

Bruce Mims: Television's sudden presence went a long way toward inspiring stations to be more locally oriented in their programming. It is what really brought about this major reemphasis on community of license.

Marvin Bensman: Local programming was strongly influenced by three factors. First, the tremendous increase in the number of new stations left more stations without network service. Second, the drastic decrease in the quantity of sponsored network programming left stations affiliated with networks with far more hours of program time to fill locally than had previously been the case. And third, increased competition among stations and much-reduced per-station revenues forced stations to look for low-cost program forms. The lowest-cost form available was that of platter programs; as a result, aside from the retention of news broadcasts and of a few talk programs, virtually all local programming was of the platter-music variety—at least by 1950. One additional comment about local radio is in order. The great success of the network telephone-quiz show, *Stop the Music,* in 1948 through 1949, resulted in a rash of local telephone-quiz programs, just as the success of the network-oriented *Major Bowes Amateur Hour* back in 1935 produced a flood of locally produced amateur-contest programs. Most of the local telephone-quiz shows had disappeared around 1951.

Gordon Hastings: Radio has always been able to react to change because it operates at the wellspring of localism and has been an industry owned and operated by broadcasters. The medium is able to feel the pulse and react quickly in great part because the nature and economics of radio programming is less cumbersome, providing for greater experimentation and development.

Stanley Hubbard: Thousands of new stations were put on the air in the fifties and sixties. The good thing about this was that it made it possible for small towns everywhere across the country to have their own local radio station. This was important because local radio stations do things that are of particular importance to their communities. Of course, the downside of all these new stations was the formidable increase in competition for advertising dollars that they created.

Ward Quaal: Around that time, radio was becoming a solid "local" medium featuring top local talent. Throughout the seventies, radio deepened its local-service emphasis.

Paul Hedberg: Indeed, local service did increase as more stations hit the airwaves, but Stan Hubbard is right about there being a downside to all the additional stations. For a good example of this, jump ahead to the 1980s when several hundred new FM stations were built as the result of the FCC's Docket 80–90. This ruling had a devastating impact on broadcasters, particularly on the local—small- and medium-size-town—level. In most cases, the big cities didn't have room for more FM stations, even before the 80–90 move. There was a glut of stations out there, and by the early nineties, sixty percent of the 80–90 FMs were losing money. The later mergers changed this.

Marvin Bensman: Mergers, cross-ownership, and intermingling into what are now transmedia companies of what once were separate businesses became the theme of this period.

James Fletcher: By the early eighties, the stage was set for a race to sell and buy radio stations, which has resulted in the rise of a number of strong companies that dominate the industry today. Many of these station groups employ satellites to program their outlets.

Marvin Bensman: The largest radio-only company in the mid-nineties was the Chancellor Media Corporation, valued at one and a half billion dollars. It owned one hundred three radio stations in twenty-one markets and held a dominant share in eleven of the twenty-five biggest radio markets—for example, fifteen percent of New York's airwaves. Only CBS radio, with annual revenues of one billion dollars, covered a bigger audience. Approximately six thousand six hundred sixty corporations and individuals owned these stations; about six hundred of these corporations owned more than one station; some one hundred forty AMs were owned by newspapers and/or magazines; one hundred sixty FM stations were owned by print media. For the average radio station, more than seventy-eight percent of sales came from local advertising.

Bruce Mims: Amid all of the high-stakes swapping in the eighties, two major initiatives signaled the FCC's reorientation of its regulatory philosophy away from the long-standing public-interest standard and toward marketplace-based decision making. In 1981, the commission's elimination of numerous documentation and operator-licensing requirements as well as the streamlining of the license-renewal process relieved broadcasters of many of their onerous record-keeping obligations. Local marketing agreements (LMAs), which consolidated the operations of two or more licensees in order to assist those stations finding it difficult to compete, became popular and were somewhat reluctantly sanctioned by the FCC.

Sam Sauls: Deregulation in the broadcasting industry introduced owners and programmers to the concept of local marketing (or management) agreements. The impact upon diversification in programming, while allowing for the sharing of resources, became a point of discussion as large companies expanded their ownership dominance within individual markets.

Lynne Gross: Deregulation, LMAs, mergers, and consolidations took hold in the eighties and would transform the medium in the coming decade and beyond.

Paul Hedberg: All of that led to the elimination of "localism" today. The idea of a community-based, local-oriented radio service became a thing of the past. The lack of "ascertainment of community needs" obligations and suggested percentages of news and public affairs programs resulted in the erosion of the approach. In the nineties, AM-FM duopoly and multiple ownership rules were obliterated. Do what you want and own what you want became the law of the land—thanks to the Telecommunications Act.

Marvin Bensman: The Telecommunications Act of 1996 permitted unlimited ownership of radio stations subject to some constraints. An individual or corporation may own up to eight radio stations in a market of forty-five or more commercial outlets; not more than five in the same service (AM or FM). In markets of thirty to forty-four stations, one may own up to seven radio stations, but not more than four in the same service. In markets with fifteen to twenty-nine stations, one may own six, but not more than four in the same service. In radio markets of fourteen or less, one may own five stations, but not more than three in the same service or more than fifty percent of the radio stations in that market. Another constraint is that same-market stations cannot duplicate programming for more than twenty-five percent of their schedules, and the Justice Department in 1996 made companies sell off stations in a market if they controlled more than forty to fifty percent of the total broadcast revenue. This was the rule of law in 1998 anyway.

Douglas Gomery: The Telecom Act of 1996 set off the greatest merger wave in history. CBS took over Infinity Broadcasting; Hicks Muse, a Dallas investment firm, acquired more than four hundred stations and formed Chancellor Media Corporation. In a telling metaphor, Infinity's founder, Mel Karmazin (later the president of CBS), noted: "It's like combining two ocean-front properties." He meant that the new empire would not be some "mom and pop" collection of rural stations in small towns, but it would own seven stations in New York City, six in Los Angeles, ten in Chicago, eight in San Francisco, and four in Washington, D.C. In the top ten markets, the new CBS combo—

had it been in place in 1995—would have commanded nearly a third of all radio advertising revenues in the country. By the mid-1990s, the radio broadcasting industry had been largely deregulated and ownership limits were all but gone.

Charles Howell: By the latter part of the decade the domination patterns were very obvious. CBS controlled more than half of all advertising dollars poured into radio in Philadelphia; a third in Boston, Dallas/Fort Worth, and Detroit; a quarter in St. Louis and Los Angeles; and a fifth in Washington/Baltimore and San Francisco. Another company, Cumulus Media, was formed in 1997 specifically to take advantage of this new landscape. It went from owning no stations at the time of its capitalization to owning one hundred ninety-five stations in small and medium markets by 1998. In a little more than a year, the company became the fifth largest group owner in the nation. A report in *Radio Ink* magazine noted that the company was "gobbling up radio stations at a record pace." In sum, the telecommunications reform in the 1990s transformed radio.

Michael Harrison: I consider the greatest threat to the continued growth of talk radio as an effective and productive medium for social progress and well-being to be the wave of corporate media consolidation triggered by the Telecommunications Act of 1996. Designed by Congress to increase competition and diversity of ownership, it has drastically accomplished the exact opposite. As the repeal of the Fairness Doctrine marked the beginning of the modern era of talk radio, the Telecommunications Bill can very well mark the beginning of its decline.

George Sosson: I think localism, perhaps as the result of the Telecom Act, is being redefined in the smaller markets. Companies like Capstar are employing a hard-drive-based system that enables them to centralize on-air production and disc jockeys at a corporate location, thus eliminating local personalities. Although it is said that localism, which has been the bedrock of radio since the fifties, will not be negatively impacted, I cannot see how it will not be adversely affected. You simply cannot have the necessary local flavor if your personalities are voice-tracked from a thousand miles away. However, with the prices being paid for stations today, the system known as "virtual radio" becomes an economic necessity. In the larger markets I see little, if any, negative impact on localism. I recently spoke at an Internet conference and defended radio against a group of Internet radio suppliers by stating that localism is the number-one asset radio has going for it. An Internet company can stream all the music it wants, but it cannot compete with a local traffic report or a local morning show making fun of the mayor. I stand by that conviction.

McHenry Tichenor: The advent of large radio companies that own hundreds of stations comes at a time when our advertisers—the hands that feed us—are going through the same consolidation process. In my view, it is a fortunate coincidence that our industry was able to get the regulatory changes that allow us to deal with these large-scale advertisers in terms that are relevant to them. So the change in radio localism is mirrored in similar changes all across the American business landscape. But consolidation has not resulted in a diminution of the desirable attributes of localism. In fact, I would argue that the opposite has happened and will continue to happen. Consolidation has probably resulted in somewhat less local ownership, especially in the smaller markets (although in the last twenty years, many stations in every market have had out-of-market owners). While a local broadcaster may no longer own the corner station, the rise of large radio companies with publicly traded stock has meant that, more than ever before, local employees of stations have ownership through stock options, employee stock-purchase plans, and similar vehicles. Further, I believe that this more broadly based local ownership is advantageous to our local communities and the radio stations involved. Broadcasters' compact with the government includes the obligation to serve our local towns and cities of license. More important, in the fifty years that my company has been in radio, we have found that an appreciation of local tastes and concern for local issues are good business. We have found that our competitors who were indifferent to local interests have fallen by the wayside. I believe this represents Darwinian forces working to ensure that localism survives in our industry.

Gordon Hastings: The new challenge facing radio will be whether the new world of consolidation with corporate and financial ownership will make radio less adaptable and less able to respond quickly to changing market conditions. On the other hand, a consolidated industry may seize the opportunity to compete better in the vastly changed world of television. Radio's next renaissance will be determined by the stewardship of the new ownerships.

Stanley Hubbard: While the industry appears healthy and robust, I believe there are too few owners today. My thinking is that the more independent voices there are, the better. Of course, I also believe in the free marketplace, so there is little I can or would do about the consolidation and conglomeration of radio groups.

Erik Barnouw: The diminution of ownership numbers could impact diversity and inhibit creative freedom. I don't know whether it actually has done that yet, but it certainly has the potential to do so—seriously and disastrously. I discuss this to some extent in *Conglomerates and the Media.*

Pierre Bouvard: I don't think there is any real cause for alarm. The importance of diversity and localism in radio will be more crucial than ever before. The medium stands at a unique point in its history. For the first time in seventy-five years, radio is being changed by alternative sources of audio. Radio is entering the world of "new media." With the advent of digital-satellite radio and audio through the Internet, the necessity of enhancing and maintaining the local-service aspects of a radio station is more important than ever.

Ward Quaal: Well, the jury is still out as to the long-lasting impact of the massive mergers and acquisitions stemming from the "freedom"-to-expand concept as set forth in the Telecommunications Act of 1996.

Sign-off:

Keep reaching for the stars!

—Casey Kasem

23

In the Air Ahead

The Future of Radio

Seems radio is here to stay.
—Norman Corwin

Radio did not exist as a mass medium at the start of the last century, yet it ultimately transformed the social and cultural landscape of the era. The first electronic mass medium altered the way Americans entertained and informed themselves. Radio's ethereal waves shrank the world and became an integral part of the waking hours of almost every man, woman, and child. The "radio music box" (as RCA's David Sarnoff called it in his prescient memo proposing the launch of the age of broadcasting) made the world laugh as well as gasp, cheer as well as mourn. It thrilled, cajoled, and comforted its loyal constituents.

"Five sets in every household," boasted the Radio Advertising Bureau. "More radios than bathtubs in the U.S.," proclaimed the textbooks used to train future radio professionals. Cue to the start of the twenty-first century, and radio does exist this time out. Yet whether its still sonorous signals will traverse the full expanse of the new millennium's first century is anybody's guess and an interesting question to ponder—as are all that deal with the unknown.

Maybe a more practical, and perhaps answerable, question to consider is what will the next decade or two have in store for radio, considering the explosion of new communication media and the veritable torrent of transfiguring technologies. Will radio, the senior citizen of the airwaves, go the way of the horse and buggy as the human race single-mindedly and often feverishly pursues the "next great thing" in communication devices, or will it, as Shakespeare put it, "live a thousand years of usefulness?"

Karl Haas: I'm really baffled as to what the future holds for radio. However, I think the need for it won't change a whole lot. People will continue to be on the go in their cars, at work, and other places where they won't be able to watch a screen, so radio will provide a valuable service in the many years to come.

Richard C. Hottelet: Despite all the new and evolving technologies, like the Internet, for example,—with its endless drizzle of factoids— radio will continue pretty much as it has. People are still going to tune in on their way to work no matter how advanced technology gets, at least in the foreseeable future. Local stations perform a unique service that will remain in demand. Traffic reports, weather updates, stock finals, sports scores, and news headlines will continue to have an audience. This kind of radio is service oriented and of continuing value.

Herbert Howard: As radio broadcasting moves into the twenty-first century, one looks back on the eighty-year history of a remarkable communications medium. From its beginning, radio has combined the elements of an engineering marvel with the ingredients of outstanding programming to create something quite extraordinary. The medium has progressed from a local curiosity to a national mass medium and ultimately back to a diversified local communication service providing a multitude of offerings.

Charles Howell: Radio is easy to use, ubiquitous, inexpensive, and filled with choices. It will be around a good long time and will no doubt play a significant role in this new millennium.

Ed Shane: In the age of one-on-one experience in cyberspace, radio seems too inclusive, too broad. Our unifying experiences are few and far between now. There's little that everyone talks about and connects with—or through. Fortunately, I still hear teenagers say that they call their friends at night to remind them to listen to the "top ten at ten" and to track all the hot new hits. That's the best news radio can have—that there's a generation ready to continue listening. I have worried that "screenagers" raised on computers and online interactivity would be sheltered from the radio experience and not be available to take over as the listeners of the future.

LeRoy Bannerman: Radio in 2000 proffers continued significance as a service medium, catering always to the interests of the local community.

Pierre Bouvard: Absolutely true. In a survey Arbitron conducted, listeners were asked what they most wanted to tune in to in the world of hundreds of station options—many of them out-of-market signals—and the overwhelming majority indicated a preference for locally programmed stations. This hasn't changed nor is it likely to change in the future.

Dick Clark: Even though radio has become diversified and audiences fractionalized, it is still one of the most important means of bringing musical material to the attention of buyers. This is another thing that has remained a constant.

Tim Powell: I'm afraid 2000 promises to be another horrible year for current music that has any interest for adults. If we ever needed to find entertainment in rock music, in the true sense of the needs of the audience, it's NOW! Multistation groups in big markets should take the core—prime demographics—and go at them from two angles: Wimpy and Bluto. End the myth of a nonexistent post-fifty hard-rock audience. Just a preference for the wall of sound over the wall of noise.

Norman Corwin: Of course, radio will never again have the front-and-center position it once occupied, but it is not now just a stiff lying behind an arras. Notwithstanding the noxious self-appointed oracles, the plethora of call-in trash, the breathlessly excited commercials, endless transmissions of inane recorded music, and a high incidence of carousel operations in which disc jockey palaver, station identifications, time signals, and other staples of day-in-day-out programming are remanded to revolving reels of tape, there are signs of life out there—principally in public radio, that is—in programs like *All Things Considered, Morning Edition, This American Life, Market Place, Car Talk, Sound Print, The Savvy Traveler;* the documentary and musical work of WBEZ, Chicago; Minnesota Public Radio; KCRW and KUSC, Los Angeles; WETA, Washington; WNEW and WNYC, New

York; WBUR and WGBH, Boston; the productions of Mary Beth Kirchner, Jay Allison, and the late *Rabbit Eras;* the special radio events of the bicoastal Museum of Television and Radio; and the active benevolence of benefactors like the Corporation for Public Broadcasting, the Ahmanson, Pew, and MacArthur Foundations, and Ralph Guild. The supply of ducats for serious radio is a trickle compared to the oceans of funding that float television, but then the senior medium no longer seeks ratings with the same ferocity it once did. Invariably the consumers of the greatest literature, drama, and music constitute a minority audience. There is nothing new or strange about that, as it is the world's experience that quality has always been, is, and always will be, an acquired taste. So relax and enjoy what we've got.

Dick Orkin: The potential to reinvigorate the "theater of the mind" in radio is not gone entirely, but it is fading into the far and distant past.

Stan Freberg: It would take some wealthy patrons to resurrect it. Radio will have a future beyond what it is now only if some benefactors—rich companies like Microsoft, for instance—realize that nothing is being done in commercial radio to enrich minds and make them think. If some of their great resources could go toward fully realizing the medium's potential, then radio in the future would be great once again and the public would truly benefit.

Ed Shane: In the foreword to the textbook *The Radio Station,* by Michael Keith, I welcomed readers to "the Golden Age of Radio." I defined the "Golden Age" as a point in the future, not in the past. The new golden age will be as meaningful as all those past periods that have been dubbed "golden ages" and revered by broadcasters nostalgic for something they cannot retrieve. Anyone who has worked for any length of time will identify a golden age. For some, it's the heyday of the radio comedian or the era of the radio drama. For others it's the top-forty era when the disc jockey and Elvis were equally called "king." The beginnings of FM are also considered a golden age. And no owner or account executive could fail to call the exponential incomes of the last few years a golden age. In Keith's book I wrote, "The next Golden Age will be created by how we use radio's unique attribute—portability—in a wired world."

Paul Harvey: I bristle a little bit when I hear people talk about the golden age of radio, because today *is* the golden age. If I had a product to sell and wanted to get the most bang for my buck, I would sponsor radio news. The medium these days is infinitely more powerful than it was, certainly per dollar, for selling most products.

Ralph Guild: Things are looking good. I think the return of national personalities and formats reflects the medium's relevancy in a changing cultural environment. Radio is still at the top of its game in so many respects.

Robert Mahlman: The medium has a wide range of national radio networks from which to choose and will have even more choices in the future. Station owners and managers continue to search for ways to operate at lower cost and continue to seek quality programming that fits their formats and demographic objectives. The major groups that have consolidated large numbers of stations under one ownership and are public have increased pressure on their station managers to increase the bottom line in order to affect their stock prices. Meanwhile, small- to medium-size-market station owners have taken advantage of the many choices by radio networks to decrease costs and not sacrifice quality programming. Today's networks provide news, weather, sports, complete music formats, and talk programs—long form and short form. It is possible to program a radio station using only programming provided by radio networks twenty-four hours a day, seven days a week. Radio networks continue to explore ways to gain and keep affiliates. Future networks and new services will expand, I believe, to provide research, sales training, inventory control, accounting, management/consulting, programming consulting, engineering equipment and services, and personnel training. In other words, future network services will grow beyond providing programming in an effort to attract affiliates, fill a need at a station, and perhaps find new sources of revenue for services and equipment needed by a station.

Ward Quaal: These network services have done well and will continue to do well. They will be major providers of programming and other station services for a long time to come.

Howard K. Smith: Well, there still is plenty of room for them to improve their programming quality, especially in the news area. I should think if radio found commentators of the caliber of those of the past, the medium would attract back some more serious listeners.

Joe Cortese: There's always room for improvement and higher quality. I think there will be more opportunities for really talented air people in the future.

Shel Swartz: You know something, I think American radio is the best in the world, and I don't think that is going to change in the years ahead.

Frank Tavares: One thing seems certain: Identifying, targeting, and reaching specific listeners will be easier. Audience research, with its increasingly sophisticated measurement techniques and use of demographics and psychographics, will provide more information about the audience. And it will provide that information in ways that become increasingly useful to programmers and beneficial to listeners. It won't stop there either. Audience (plural) research will truly become listener (singular) research. As research techniques advance and increase in reliability, those providing radio (or audio) services will become increasingly sophisticated about the listening habits and needs of individual listeners and will be able to provide programming and services for *each* listener.

Michael Harrison: We stand on the verge of a rapid intensification and definition of what are loosely referred to as "new media." The Internet is going to become the dominant platform from which all other media are derived. Thus, what we commonly thought of in the twentieth century as "radio," "television," "telephone," "records," and "movies" will be interrelated elements of the Internet. The interactivity of this medium will mark its heightened level of effectiveness. Therefore, when we look back on this era, say twenty-five years from now, talk radio of 2000 will be viewed as the primitive public address system heralding the arrival of twenty-first-century electronic-age democracy.

Walter Cronkite: I think that radio in the future might turn out to be, at least in some way, an adjunct to the Internet. While the Internet itself will be carrying pictures—it is today and will be vastly expanding that capacity in the future—I think the spoken word combined with the printed word may provide a new form of communication that will have some importance for us.

Peter Wolf: Frankly, I think the future of radio *is* the Internet. A local station can become global.

Frank Tavares: Radio distribution methods will become increasingly intelligent and able to determine the listening patterns and preferences of audience members. The medium will ultimately have the capacity to be programmed for each individual listener. Radio technology will become more intelligent. Rather than listeners having to adapt to radio's limitations, radio will adapt itself to the listener.

Sam Sauls: Digital audio broadcasting [DAB] will offer listeners crystal-clear transmission, as well as other features, in just a handful of years.

W.A. Kelly Huff: DAB will replace traditional analog radio. It is an audio signal offering compact-disc sound quality and can be transmitted to consumers in-band over existing AM and FM frequencies and/or by satellite. While some broadcasters see DAB as a threat to their existence, most see it as a way to help radio prosper. DAB also offers improved stereo and reduction of signal interference and fading.

Rick Ducey: The question as to how technology will change the radio medium is one I constantly consider in my job at the NAB. History teaches us that technology is about applications. Nobody thinks about why a light bulb brightens when the switch is flipped. Most people don't care if it is an incandescent or fluorescent light. They just want to be able to see in the dark. Technology now provides options for receiving "radio" programming via the Internet, satellites, cable systems, mobile telephony, and more in both analog and digital form. Ultimately, what people want is what they want. It is a simple premise but one that keeps the over-ten–thousand radio stations in the United States constantly challenged and competitively engaged to research and understand the psychology of their listener's needs, motives, and interests and then program to this standard. The answer varies by local, regional, and national tastes. No two stations sound the same for long. Technology could enable each of us to connect on demand to a huge audio-file server for downloading files or streaming content in real-radio listening will be the key to radio's survival. This time is ipe for syndication of some great, new radio talent.

Dees: Radio has an eternal, timeless quality. Nothing paints a e in your mind the way it does. A while back, I gushed about my l over the air—something about Ellen K's tight, pink sweater and eat-locker temperatures in the studio. Ellen said, "I got this er at half price!" and I countered with, "And you got it half on!" losed the segment with "Tight, pink sweaters do strange things in er like this." There is no more personal relationship than that of orning radio host and the listener. As the world wakes up, it s me into its bedroom, its bathroom, its car, and those sacred t places in its life. Why would that change, even in a hundred ?

Owens: Radio is healthier than ever. Whoever thought that radio would go for two thousand dollars in a single market? Let's pray here will always be room for all kinds of formats and diversity. giant demographic pie. I personally have been blessed to work y every format: middle-of-the-road, top forty, jazz, country, adult mporary, sports, news, yodeling, ethnic weather—every one is a . radio is a joy!

y Gelbart: Well, unless there is some original programming— ust news, talk, call-ins, and recorded music (yodeling notwith- ing)—radio will continue, despite all these new technologies, to st an outbox filled mostly with prattle (except for Garrison Keil- nd the same old same old.

off:

ou on the radio.

—Charles Osgood

time. However, that requires a lot of work fr
there will be times when we want to hear so
President Clinton's testimony in the Kenneth St
ever, most of the time it turns out that the audi
to listen to a program director's selection of of
familiar with the occasional surprise. Technolo
the way radio needs to recognize and serve its a
is more frustrating than to arrive at work and
machine what a great interview Don Imus had
and not be able to hear it? Wouldn't it be gre
connect to the station's Web site, and hear it fo
cut you heard on your favorite music station—
what was the name of the new CD? Go to the st
these questions, and perhaps make a purchase c
load the digital content directly or have a CD
Technology will increase the options audience
with content they care about. This will both co
ences. Radio stations will embrace the same t
petitors do to continue serving and begin
audiences and advertisers. Technology will ma
brilliant. It will allow stations the opportunity t
create communities of common interest in real
communities of interest in any time.

Corey Flintoff: Programming will become n
Technology will allow us to serve more and
ences and, in many cases, to serve them interac
be less of an issue, because listeners will be
when they're ready for them, not just at one
Programming will be more of an issue. Instea
product to capture bigger audiences, we'll ha
selves more, be more original, more interesting.

Richard Fatherley: I think, in part due to all
the standard-wave AM band to disappear, follo
move to UHF frequencies. Radio service will b
sion with computer-retrievable digital audio.

Arnie Ginsburg: Radio programming in this
tinue to be driven by demographics and availat

Aut
still

Rick
pictt
frien
the
swe
She
wea
the
allo
secr
year

Gar
spot
that
It's
near
cont
joy .

Lar
not
stan
be j
lor)

Sign

See

24

Seems Radio Is Here to Stay by Norman Corwin

A Play for Broadcast

The script that follows is offered as an appropriate and fitting epilogue to this book's narrative and an exemplar of the highly literary and innovative nature of golden-age radio drama, wherein the "word" was, indeed, the thing. Simply reading it—without the intended accompaniment of deftly crafted and sculpted sounds—is convincing enough evidence that this short-lived art form was something rare and special. Hundreds of original verse and prose plays were written and produced for the radio networks, and while not all aspired to or achieved greatness, many certainly warranted the outpouring of critical praise they received at the time of their broadcasts.

This radio drama was first aired over CBS on April 24, 1939. For publication in this book, Mr. Corwin updated his play.

NARRATOR:	Do we come on you unaware,
	Your set untended?
	Do you put down your paper to raise an ear,
	Suspend what you were just about to say
	Or stay the finger that could snap shut
	The traps of night between us?
	Were you expecting us?
	Your dial deputized to let us in
	At thirty minutes after ten along the seaboard on the east,

Nine-thirty inland by a thousand miles,
A mountain's half-past eight,
And dinner dishes still uncleared on shores that face Japan?

In any case, good evening or good afternoon, good morning
    or good night,
Whichever best becomes the sector of the sky
Arched over your antenna.
We wish some words with you
Concerning magic that would make a
Merlin envious.
The miracle, worn ordinary now, of just such business as
    this
Between your ears and us, and oceantides of ether.
We mean the genii of radio
Kowtowing to Aladdins everywhere,
As flashy on the run as light, and full of services to ships at
    sea and planes in the air and people in their living
    rooms, resembling you.

All this by way of prologue
And prologues should not be prolonged.
Let our announcer do what he's engaged to do:
Announce what this is all about.
And let there be, when he is done, some interest expressed
By brasses and by strings.
A little music, let us say,
To start an introspective program on its way.

*Bring in oscillator, with stream of code in definite rhythmic pattern; then bring in
second oscillator at lower pitch and with contrapuntal rhythmic pattern. Hold
both until:*

*Music: Orchestra picks up pitch and tempi of both oscillators and develops material
into a fanfare.*

NARRATOR: That will take care of overtures and prologues for tonight.
                             You'd think that we were warming up
                             To something steamy in the way of melodrama
                             Magniloquent with love and hate, sacrifice and
                                 sin, repentance, and with sound effects
                             But no—
                             But none of that—
                             As we said before,
                             We're here to talk of radio.

                             Let's start by setting forth
                             That it is good to take a nip of fancy every now and then

A swig or two of wonderment to jog the mind,
Excursioning beyond too well-worn thoughtscapes
If only as a form of exercise—
Especially in times like these, when
    headlines blaze their blackest,
And thunders grumble, and the skies darken with forecasts
    of distress.
It purges toxins
To think away from crises,
To think that even for man's monkeying with mania and
    murder
He's still an authentic walking phenomenon
Bound round by marvels.

Do you remember what it was that Whitman said about
    miracles?
Come in, Walt Whitman, and remind us:

Music: Passage behind:

WHITMAN: I believe a leaf of grass is no less than the journey-work of
(on filter mike)   the stars,
                    And the narrowest hinge in my hand puts to scorn all
                      machinery,
                    And the cow crunching with depress'd head surpasses any
                      statue.
                    And a mouse is miracle enough to stagger sextillions of
                      infidels.

Music: Fade behind:

NARRATOR: You call these wonders, Whitman?
                    Well, they are. And we agree
                    They put to scorn machinery,
                    And yet no mouse in Vermont, by
                      his own talents,
                    Ever squeaked a squeak
                    Heard in Australia
                    Nor can a cow moo in a three-way conversation
                    With two other cows in distant pasture lands.
                    Here is machinery for you, Walt,
                    To tease the imaginings of all the poets in the world.
                    We speak of the dials, filaments, and microphones,
                    The crystals, coils,
                    And towers that inject the sky
                    With ectoplasms of sound and speech and music
                    The innards of your receiver
                    Selecting, sifting strands of ether, letting pass
                    That only which it pleases you to hear.

Let's see the gods do better!
Dare they vie
With engineers of radio?
It is to laugh!
The fulminating thunderclaps of Jove
Are faint mumblings just a country's breadth away,
Whereas the mildest microphonic whisperings,
Like this . . .

WHISPERER: Hello, Antipodes!

NARRATOR: . . . Go spinning round the globe
Not once, but seven times
Within the twinkling of a mouse's eye,
And on their way unswerved by winds,
Dissolving in no mists,
Undrowned in deeps
And never tangled in a jungle's tracery.
Nor can the frowning Himalayas, range on range,
Even momentarily intimidate our whispering.
The Himalayas, did we say?
Why, the earth itself, the planet underfoot, is even solider,
And yet . . .

WHISPERER: Hello, Antipodes!

NARRATOR: . . . thrusts through the earth as clean
As would a guillotine
Through cheesecake.
Indeed, the ground has ears!
Perhaps, for all we know,
This is telephony with *buried* listeners.
If all a planet's denseness
Cannot stop our whisperings,
Will then mere coffin walls?
We'll make our microphones directional
And speak to whom we please.

(Calling)   O BEETHOVEN!
O LUDWIG!
HAVE YOU GOT YOUR HEARING BACK?
WE CALL YOUR HALLOWED BONES!

Do we disturb your rest?

Death is too long a leisure, we suspect,
For one of such invention.
You must be out assembling harmonies somewhere.
But listen, maestro; hear:

Music: Sneak in the opening movement of Beethoven's Fifth Symphony. Bring up gradually under:

NARRATOR:

There are more ears attending you tonight
Than ever you imagined could perceive a note:
And all at once: this instant.
More by millions than ever gathered
In continents of concert halls.
Your music gets around these days.
On plains, on mountains, and on shores
    you never heard of,
You are heard tonight.

Your music beats against a sounding board of stars;
It flows in raptures down spillways of space;
It sweeps, precisely in the
    figuration you set down,
Across immensity.

Music: Up full to conclusion.

NARRATOR:

You see, Beethoven?
You have not been changed
By so much as a hemidemisemiquaver!

Let's turn our microphone
And stir some sacred dust in Stratford:

O SHAKESPEARE!
WILLIAM SHAKESPEARE!
WE ARE CALLING FROM A LAND YOU'D LIKE TO
    BE ACQUAINTED WITH:
FOUR DOZEN FEDERATED STATES IN NORTH
    AMERICA,
NOT FAR FROM THOSE BERMUDAS THAT YOU
    WROTE ABOUT!

Here are new Venices and Elsinores,
New Athenses and Troys,
New Englands and New Londons and New Yorks

Where you are better known than all the kings in Britain's
history!
Your language trips upon the tongues of
schoolboys, lovers, soldiers, justices
And lean and slippered pantaloons.
You stand with Bibles on our shelves
And are as often quoted as a savior:

FIRST MAN: Aha, hanging is too good for him.

SECOND MAN: Well, you have to give the devil his due.

FIRST WOMAN: The course of true love never did run smooth.

THIRD MAN: It was Greek to me.

SECOND WOMAN: He eats me out of house and home!

THIRD WOMAN: Why don't you send him packing?

FIRST MAN: It's a wise father that knows his own son.

SECOND MAN: I pause for a reply.

THIRD MAN: It smells to heaven.

FIRST MAN: I'll tell the world.

SECOND MAN: Sweets to the sweet.

THIRD WOMAN: I am nothing if not critical.

FIRST MAN: Dead as a doornail.

SECOND MAN: Neither rhyme nor reason.

SECOND WOMAN: Uneasy lies the head that wears the crown.

NARRATOR: Three centuries ago
They put you in a tomb.
Since then the world has writhed and floundered
And generals have died in peace.
And peaceful populations died in war,
And arts and attitudes and ancient gods decayed—
And yet there's not a trace of mold about your poetry

Far less so now than ever, for the theater has grown
To take in all the stages of the land
All villages and hamlets
Cabins hard to get to
Houses high on hills, and islands where the ferry plies but
    once a week,
Lone trapper in the woods
And ranger on the range
And lighthouse-keeper polishing his glass
They all can hear you now within the compass of this voice.
Your audience has grown
All modern actors want to play your Hamlet.
These much-minded Americans wish hotly to personify a
    royal Dane.
Who are we to stand between
Ambition and the act?
One plays him now
A fragment passionate and murderous.
Attend, for Hamlet enters now the closet of the queen.
Polonius is hid behind the arras:

HAMLET: Now, Mother, what's the matter?

QUEEN: Hamlet, thou hast thy father much offended.

HAMLET: Mother, you have my father much offended.

QUEEN: Come, come, you answer with an idle tongue.

HAMLET: Go, go, you question with a wicked tongue.

NARRATOR: *(over the dialogue, which is reduced by the engineer on the control board).*

This *Hamlet* was not advertised tonight, and yet a multitude is listening.

More than they accommodate at the Globe in London

And none sits in the balcony.

The seats of radio are Row A center
And the tickets always complimentary.

QUEEN: Why, how now, Hamlet?

HAMLET: What's the matter now?

QUEEN: Have you forgot me?

HAMLET: No, by the rood, not so:
You are the queen, your husband's
    brother's wife;
And—would it were not so!—you
    are my mother.

QUEEN: Nay then, I'll set those to you that can speak.

HAMLET: Come, come, and sit down; you shall not budge;
You go not, till I set you up a glass
Where you may see the inmost part of you.

QUEEN: What wilt thou do? thou wilt not murder me?
                                Help, help, ho!

POLONIUS: *(off)*.   Help! Help! Help!

HAMLET: How now! a rat? Dead, for a ducat, dead!
(sound of drawing; off).

POLONIUS: O! I am slain.

QUEEN: O me! what has thou done?

HAMLET: Nay, I know not: is it the king?

QUEEN: O! what a rash and bloody deed is this!

HAMLET: A bloody deed! almost as bad, good Mother,
                                As kill a king and marry with his brother.

QUEEN: As kill a king!

HAMLET: 'Twas my word . . .
                                Leave wringing of your hands: peace! sit you down,
                                And let me wring your heart; for so I shall
                                If it be made of penetrable stuff

NARRATOR: You were an actor, Will.
You know a play does not spring suddenly
    from floor boards unrehearsed
Or drop full-blown and edited from
    heaven
It must be written first, then cast:;
Directed and produced
And when it's done by radio
It must be engineered.
How else can Hamlet rant in Honolulu
As he rants right here?
This is a question for the engineers.
Their language has a listenable cadence of its
    own;
To wit:

ENGINEER: I'm getting a low-frequency tone.
    Will you check to see where it's coming
    from?

SECOND ENGINEER: The S.E. filter is set for
    cutoff at two-hundred cycles.

If damned custom have
        not brass'd it so
    That it is proof and bulwark
        against sense.

QUEEN: What have I done that thou
        dar'st wag thy tongue
    In noise so rude against me?

HAMLET: Such an act
That blurs the grace and blush of
    modesty
Calls virtue hypocrite, takes off the
    rose
From the fair forehead of an
    innocent love
And sets a blister there, makes
    marriage vows
As false as dicers' oaths; O! such a
    deed
As from the body of contraction
    plucks
The very soul, and sweet religion
    makes

THIRD ENGINEER: Smithers reporting. Studio 3. Ten-thirty to eleven P.M. Here's your test.

FOURTH ENGINEER: "Seems Radio:" sustaining, going local, New York State, north round robin, except RR5; Dixie, RR19; CBX.

A rhapsody of words;
  heaven's face doth
  glow
Yea, this solidity and compound
  mass,
With trustful visage as against the
  doom,
Is thought-sick at the act.

QUEEN: Ay me! what act,
That roars so loud and thunders in
  the index?

HAMLET: Look here, upon this
  picture, and on this;
The counterfeit presentment of two
  brothers.

See, what a grace was seated on this brow;
Hyperion's curls, the front of Jove himself;
An eye like Mars, to threaten and command,
A station like the herald Mercury
New-lighted on a heaven-kissing hill,
A combination and a form indeed,
Where every god did seem to set his seal,
To give the world assurance of a man.
This was your husband: look you now,
  what follows.

NARRATOR: Poor Hamlet, he has never been so interrupted
He is making such a scene behind our engineers
  It seems a pity to obtrude.
Obtrude?
Why, come to think of it, our Smithers has more
  venom at his finger tips
Than Laertes on his sword.
The turning of a dial can efface our Hamlet
  quicker
Than the most incisive foil.
Stand by to hear a Dane evaporate:

Here is your husband; like a
  mildew'd ear,
Blasting his wholesome brother.
  Have you eyes?
Could you on this fair mountain
  leave to feed,
And batten on this moor? Ha! have
  you eyes?
You cannot call it love, for at your
  age
The hey-day in the blood is tame,
  it's humble,
And waits upon the judgment; and
  what judgment
Would step from this to this?
  Sense, sure, you have

Else could you not have motion, but sure, that sense *(fading)*
Is apoplex'd; for madness would not err,

>   Nor sense to ecstasy was ne'er so thrall'd
>   But it reserv'd some quantity of choice,
>   To serve in such a difference . . .

Hamlet is faded.

NARRATOR: Go, rest now, Hamlet
                       You've been around the world and back
                       And in a million homes
                       And in the tomb of him who gave you utterance.
                       We've faded you and been discourteous, and that's enough.
                       So thanks; so long; good-bye;
                       We'll meet again some day
                       In some such studio as this.
                       A little music, please,
                       For a departing royal gentleman.

Music; Flourish for Hamlet departure.

NARRATOR: There is some delicacy in the fact
                       That all things delicate were once exceeding crude:
                       Language can be traced to croaking frogs,
                       Sweet scents to vomiting of whales;
                       The raw material of men is dust
                       Of diamonds, lampblack.
                       The vast mainsprings of Time
                       Which keep the very stars to their appointments
                       Were forged no doubt out of some coarse galactic ore.
                       But here's the point we're getting to:
                       That radio itself, so delicately tuned and timed,
                       Transmitted and received,
                       Is, too, compounded of base clay and perspiration,
                       Plans and graphs and conferences,
                       Instruments and agencies whose labor is
                             unheard, unseen, unsung.
                       They serve the industry and you
                       With intimacies equal to the service of the trunk unto the
                             tree;
                       The twist unto the hand.

The following speeches cross-fade into each other.

CABINET MAKER: I make cabinets for radio sets, and when the season's good . . .

SALES REPRESENTATIVE: I'm a national sales representative of sixteen of the country's
                       biggest stations . . .

ACTOR: I was picked out of fifty from the audition. It's a contract for twenty-six weeks. Of course, they won't let me have any conflicts, but considering the terms . . .

WORKER: I am engaged in the manufacture of water coils and porcelain pipe for carrying water to radio tubes in transmitting stations. We turn out an average of . . .

ATTORNEY: As a lawyer practicing before the Federal Communications Commission, I represent applicants for licenses to own and operate . . .

GIRL: Yes, sir. I will have this report typed up in about five minutes.

SALESMAN: We make the finest antenna impedance matching units and dielectric capacitators in the business . . .

AGENT: I got an estimate on talent costs, director, music, sound, scripts, and rights. It sounds like a good show to buy.

SCRUBWOMAN: I come in at ten every night and wash the floors on the
(Slavic accent)   fifteenth and sixteenth floors, sometimes also on the seventeenth.

DIRECTOR: Sound, bring up the train effect behind the narrator, and don't start fading until after cue ninety-four on page twenty-three. Mr. Carpenter, will you please work a little closer to the mike in your scene with Miss Kent . . .

EDUCATOR: And we're adding to the curriculum for the spring term a course on radio writing by the head of the script division . . .

RECORDING: Okay, I'll start to cut on phone cue from you.

Music: Instruments tuning up.

CONDUCTOR: All right, gentlemen. Now take it from the letter C—ten, eleven, twelve measures, and I'd like a little more brass, please, and heavier afterbeats. All right?

Rap of baton.
Music: Popular tune; bring down and fade slowly under:

FIRST VOICE: Deals, overtime put in,
Wages and hours, clauses in the
   contracts,
Floors scrubbed, phone calls answered,
Memoranda written, figures added up,
Pay checks distributed,
Inquiries and answers

SECOND VOICE: Budget, copyright release,
                   Timeclock, elevator guard
                   Yes and no and sorry-try-again
                   The date for lunch
                   The swell idea
                   The new man coming in next Monday
                   The program ending on the nose

THIRD VOICE: Transmitter tone
                   And resin for the bow
                   And sales gone up by twenty-two per cent

FOURTH VOICE: Air conditioning and dividends
                       Stocks on the exchange . . .

NARRATOR: You who sit at home or ride in cars
                   Or hear us on a Walkman:
                   You are the critic and the judge
                   The twister of the knob
                   You rule the wavelengths by selection.
                   You like it *this* way?
                   This way it shall be.
                   You like it *that?*
                   Then that.
                   We do not send our signals to the moon
                   But target *you* and watch to see if we have made a hit.

FIRST LISTENER: I like this kind of a program, but my wife doesn't. She
                       prefers drama and variety.

SECOND LISTENER: Well, I don't care much for variety, but I sure love sports
                       and talk shows.

FIRST WOMAN: The classical music station. It's on day and night.
                   When I can't sleep it sweetens my insomnia.

SECOND WOMAN: I've been following the serial that comes on right
                       after the news in the morning.

THIRD MAN: Give me rock.

THIRD WOMAN: My little boy always wanted to hear that cowboy program at dinnertime, but his sister quarreled with him because she insisted on hearing *The Claghorns,* so I finally got another radio to keep the peace in the family. My husband likes politics and call-in shows, which I can't stand. Well, everybody's entitled to his own opinion, I always say.

NARRATOR: Thank God for differences!
Let opinions be as varied and as free to come and go as weather is—
Like wind, spontaneous; like storm, forthright.
The saying is that difference of opinion makes the world go round,
And that's a platitude you tip your hat to when you meet it.
You'll find, wherever viewpoints must be such-and-such or else,
And opinion's smuggled out like contraband,
In such a place the world stops short and goes around no more.
The world stands still because it is *afraid* to move.
The air we listen to must be as free as that we breathe
Or there will rise such dissonance and cacophony
As will stave in the eardrum!

Music: Spirited passage; soften under:

NARRATOR: The race of man is shrewd and silly, brutal and benign
And full of sudden starts and tardy reckonings.
One day, when all the menacing is done with
And a man can wish another well across a border,
His speech will sweeten;
He will cast abroad such sentiments
As *should* be radiated in the skies.

Do you grant radio is here to stay?
Then grant this further:
That the ethers were established well before the first word passed between two men:
It's only latterly we've seen that speech is buoyant in these waves;
There may this very moment be,
As close to us as one discoverer away,
Whole firmaments of stuffs awaiting comprehension.

That we'll see about.

Meanwhile some homage to the High Commissioner
Who first assigned these frequencies to earth,
Who marked these airlanes out.
He is the same Who fixed the stars in place,
Who set afire the sun and froze the moon and dug the
    furrows wherein oceans flow.
He holds the formula for genesis and death.
His hand rests on a dial bigger than infinity.
This microphone is not an ordinary instrument,
For it looks out on vistas wide indeed:
My voice commingles now with northern lights and
    asteroids and Alexander's skeleton,
With dead volcanoes and with donkey's ears.
It swims with minnows, and it's in the Sphinx's jaw.
It drifts among whatever spirits pass across the night.
Here is a thought to fasten to your throat:
Who knows who may be listening? And where?

Music: Conclusion

Epilogue: Seems Radio *Is* Here to Stay

As reported by the *New York Times* on June 3, 1999:

> Americans bought more than 58 million radios for the home last year.
> In fact, the Consumer Electronics Manufacturers Association reports
> that most homes have at least eight of them. If car radios are in-
> cluded, that number rises to 9 or 10 per home, making radios easily the
> most ubiquitous consumer electronics device in the nation.[*]

---

[*]Joel Brinkley, p. E1.

Further Reading

Allen, Steve. *Hi-Ho Steverino!* Ft. Lee, NJ: Barricade Books, 1992.

Barfield, Ray. *Listening to Radio: 1920–1950.* Westport, CT: Praeger, 1996.

Barlow, William. *Voice Over: The Making of Black Radio.* Philadelphia: Temple University Press, 1999.

Barnouw, Erik. *The Image Empire: A History of Broadcasting in the United States.* Vol. 3. New York: Oxford University Press, 1970.

Bliss, Ed. *Now the News.* New York: Columbia University Press, 1991.

Delong, Thomas A. *The Mighty Music Box.* Los Angeles: Amber Crest Books, 1980.

Ditingo, Vincent M. *The Remaking of Radio.* Boston: Focal Press, 1996.

Douglas, Susan J. *Listening In.* New York: Times Books, 1999.

Dunning, John. *On the Air: The Encyclopedia of Old-Time Radio.* New York: Oxford University Press, 1998.

Fang, Irving. *Those Radio Commentators.* Ames: Iowa State University Press, 1977.

Fong-Torres, Ben. *The Hits Just Keep On Coming.* San Francisco: Miller Freeman Books, 1998.

Fornatale, Peter, and Joshua Mills. *Radio in the Television Age.* New York: Overlook Press, 1980.

Hall, Claude, and Barbara Hall. *The Business of Radio Programming.* New York: Hastings House, 1978.

Halper, Donna. *Full-Service Radio.* Boston: Focal Press, 1991.

Hilliard, Robert, and Michael Keith. *The Broadcast Century.* Boston: Focal Press, 1997.

———. *Waves of Rancor.* Armonk, NY: M.E. Sharpe, 1999.

Hilmes, Michele. *Radio Voices: American Broadcasting, 1922–1952.* Minneapolis: University of Minnesota Press, 1997.

Keith, Michael C. *Radio Programming: Consultancy and Formatics.* Boston: Focal Press, 1987.

———. *Signals in the Air.* Westport, CT: Praeger, 1995.

———. *Voices in the Purple Haze.* Westport, CT: Praeger, 1997.

———. *The Radio Station.* 5th ed. Boston: Focal Press. Forthcoming.

Ladd, Jim. *Radio Waves*. New York: St. Martin's Press, 1991.

Langguth, A.J., ed. *Norman Corwin's Letters*. New York: Barricade Books, 1994.

Lewis, Tom. *Empire of the Air*. New York: Harper-Collins, 1991.

Looker, Thomas. *The Sound and the Story*. Boston: Houghton Mifflin, 1995.

Lujack, Larry, and D.A. Jedlicka. *Superjock*. Chicago: Regnery, 1975.

MacDonald, J. Fred. *Don't Touch That Dial*. Chicago: Nelson Hall, 1979.

MacFarland, David T. *The Development of the Top 40 Format*. New York: Arno Press, 1979.

Maltin, Leonard. *The Great American Broadcast*. New York: Dutton, 1997.

Morrow, Bruce. *Cousin Brucie*. New York: Morrow, 1987.

Norberg, Eric G. *Radio Programming: Tactics and Strategy*. Boston: Focal Press, 1996.

Pease, Edward, and Everette Dennis. *Radio: The Forgotten Medium*. New Brunswick, NJ: Transaction Press, 1995.

Rhoads, Eric. *Radio's First 75 Years*. West Palm Beach, FL: Streamline Press, 1996.

Routt, Ed., and James B. McGrath. *The Radio Format Conundrum*. New York: Hastings House, 1978.

Savage, Barbara Dianne. *Broadcasting Freedom: Radio, War, and the Politics of Race*. Chapel Hill, NC: The University of North Carolina Press, 1999.

Schiffer, Michael B. *The Portable Radio in American Life*. Tucson: University of Arizona Press, 1991.

Shane, Ed. *Selling Electronic Media*. Boston: Focal Press, 1999.

Sklar, Rick. *Rocking America: How the All-Hit Stations Took Over*. New York: St. Martin's Press, 1984.

Sterling, Christopher, and John Kittross. *Stay Tuned*. 2d ed. Belmont, CA: Wadsworth, 1990.

Vowell, Sarah. *Radio On: A Listener's Diary*. New York: St. Martin's Press, 1997.

Williams, Gilbert A. *Legendary Pioneers of Black Radio*. Westport, CT: Praeger, 1998.

Index